ABUNDANT EVER AFTER

ABUNDANT EVER AFTER

Tools for Creating a Life
of Prosperity and Ease

CATHY HELLER

Simon Element

New York   London   Toronto   Sydney   New Delhi

SIMON ELEMENT

An Imprint of Simon & Schuster, LLC
1230 Avenue of the Americas
New York, NY 10020

First Simon Element hardcover edition December 2024

SIMON ELEMENT is a trademark of Simon & Schuster, LLC

Simon & Schuster: Celebrating 100 Years of Publishing in 2024

For information about special discounts for bulk purchases, please contact Simon & Schuster Special Sales at 1-866-506-1949 or business@simonandschuster.com.

The Simon & Schuster Speakers Bureau can bring authors to your live event. For more information or to book an event, contact the Simon & Schuster Speakers Bureau at 1-866-248-3049 or visit our website at www.simonspeakers.com.

Manufactured in the United States of America

10 9 8 7 6 5 4 3 2 1

Library of Congress Cataloging-in-Publication Data has been applied for.

ISBN 978-1-6680-2238-2
ISBN 978-1-6680-2240-5 (ebook)

For my daughters, Gabrielle, Eliza, and Madeleine. May you always know the power that lies within you and the love that surrounds you.

Thank you for bringing so much light to my life.

TABLE OF CONTENTS

ABUNDANT EVER AFTER

INTRODUCTION

W ELCOME. I'm so glad you're here. You've come to the right place. I'd like you to take a moment and ask yourself...

Why did you pick up this book?
What are you longing to be shown?

I believe that all the answers live within you, and if I'm successful, then the pages of this book will walk you home to yourself. There is a part of us that knows things can be simpler, more peaceful, and more fulfilling than they currently are. This book will show you how to set down the unnecessary heaviness and unlock magnificent possibilities.

I'm going to walk you through a process that helps you understand how to use the tools you have inherently been given to create the most amazing life. Imagine that your friend had a waffle iron and used it as a paperweight. She would be missing out on what could have been a lifetime of the most delicious breakfasts, all because she didn't know how to use the features of this awesome device. Think of yourself as an amazing instrument that was meant to play the most beautiful music, a Steinway piano that has sat in the living room collecting dust because you never learned how to play the keys.

Throughout the pages of this book, I will explain the major components that will help you access the greatest blessings waiting in escrow for you. You will understand your inherent connection to the divine. I will help it all make sense. You will see things through a new lens. You will become a better receiver of all the good available to you. You will realize how much love you are here to give and how good it feels to be a loving force wherever you go. This is about so much more than taking great vacations, launching a business, or achieving goals. This is about letting go of the illusion of lack and tuning into the bountiful, infinite state of the universe.

We are so married, so committed to the illusion and to the idea that the way life works is for it all to be hard. In truth, it is meant to flow and feel like ease. It is meant to come to you as synchronicity. It is meant to show up as a blessing. Everything you desire is already here, hidden in plain sight. It is already done.

None of it happens through hard work. None of it. Ask yourself, what does it feel like when your mind and body are in a state of ease? What does it feel like to love? Do you remember how to play? How good can you tolerate feeling? Imagine your life in flow. When you let go of trying so hard to figure it out and instead open your heart and realize the enormity that lives within you, you will feel a wholeness like never before. You will experience the world as a friendly place where synchronicity happens all day long. You will realize you are in the right place at the right time all the time, because when you're tuned into love, you'll feel it everywhere and you'll bring it into every room you enter and it will be all that you'll see. This leads to the most amazing opportunities, because true, authentic joy is a magnet for the miraculous; because the mystical is available every second.

You will nod along in the pages ahead because you will be reminded that there is so much in this book that you knew all along. You will start to feel happier. You will start to observe uncanny coincidences becoming a daily norm. You will have new ideas and inspired downloads, and moments of creative flow will begin to emerge. You will start taking better care of yourself and enjoying more of the little moments throughout your day. Perhaps you will feel satisfied, whole, and suddenly awake to an endless number of beautiful possibilities that are here for the taking.

One thing is for sure: you will learn that you are a soul, and you will begin to see how being connected to that is the most powerful thing you'll ever experience. You will understand how to focus your attention in a way that will allow you to imprint the most beautiful energy onto this world. And once you do, you will be Abundant Ever After.

You might not know it yet, but . . .

You are already whole.

You are already abundant.

You are already worthy.

You are already a masterpiece. A piece of the master.

1.

ABUNDANCE = BE A RECEIVER

WHEN YOU THINK of the word *abundance*, what comes to mind? Is it a pile of money? Is it a beautiful vacation home on the beach? Is it eating your favorite takeout every night? Is it a first-class plane ticket? Is it writing a check for millions of dollars to a charity? Is it being able to do what you love and getting paid well for it?

Now imagine you had those things. How does that make you *feel*?

I was raised like many people to think that abundance was a certain level of success that was achievable through hard work or luck. Every challenging conclusion people draw is that all of life is a race to see who can achieve the most. This approach has left a lot of people feeling empty and depleted. What's even worse is that the key to their own happiness was always within, and the path was so simple that they skipped right over it. Contrary to popular opinion, abundance is more than a giant bank account. Abundance isn't about money, but we have a false perception that the more money we have, the fuller we'll feel. The truth is, we didn't come into this world for a pile of things. We have much bigger dreams than that. We came for an elevated state of consciousness, a feeling of wholeness and connection. It's the feeling of inner peace, creativity, and contribution that we're really after.

You've likely heard about the law of attraction, where things that you desire are outside of you, and your job is to attract something that's at a distance from where you are now. We were taught that all we had to do was get clear on what we wanted and it would materialize. Many of us who bought into this idea are still waiting for results; we're still pining for our dreams somewhere over the rainbow and wondering *Why haven't I attracted the life I dream for myself? Why isn't it working?*

Well, what if I told you that the law of attraction may actually hold us back from allowing in more? What if it's not about attracting at all? What if the magic is in the *receiving*?

My dear teacher Rabbi David Aaron was the first to help me understand that the universe works through the law of reception. Based on the word *Kabbalah*, which means "to receive," the idea is that everything that we need and most desire in life is already here—you don't have to attract it. You just have to receive it; you just have to *allow it in*. There's nothing at a far distance from us and nothing we need to force to have it. Right here in this moment all potentials already exist, and the question is, How much do you allow yourself to receive?

When first explaining this concept to me, he used the radio as a metaphor, and I love it so much. He said a radio has the capacity to tune into music that is always here, hidden in plain sight. We are designed just like that. When we tap into our truest frequency, we experience a totally new reality. We are in charge of what appears. It all depends on which wavelength we're on. As a latchkey kid in the '80s and '90s, I had my Sony Boombox to keep me entertained. It was one of those old-school boomboxes with the rabbit ears, and depending on the day, I would manipulate those ears to tune it to pop, oldies, sometimes a rock station. A variety of music was at my fingertips, and it was up to me to tune to the station of my choosing and receive it.

Here's my way of understanding this metaphor. The whole journey here is about being a receiver. If I have a radio sitting next to me and I turn it on, I'll hear music. If the radio is off, I won't hear anything. So I turn it on. But then once I turn it on, depending on what the radio is tuned to, I might hear a salsa song. If I tune it another way, I might hear hip-hop or classical music.

So, what's in control of the broadcast? It's whatever the receiver is picking up.

When we look at it this way, we realize that all potentials exist in this quantum field. All realities exist in this moment, and the one you're in is the one you're attuned to. The experience of your life is a mirror of the radio station you have chosen. You just don't necessarily know that. But once you understand that you are in control of the music you want to broadcast and receive, you realize, *Wow. That's unbelievable. That is so empowering, I can choose a different station.*

Did you get that?

All the music is already here. You simply have to tune into a certain frequency to receive a different type of song.

This is how abundance works.

As Wayne Dyer said, "We don't get what we want, we get what we are." There is a principle in science called the law of resonance. If I were to go into a guitar shop and take one guitar off the shelf and play the D string, all the other guitars in the store would vibrate. Not only that, but it would be only the D string on the other guitars that would move in resonance to match the note I played. We literally get back the signal we send out. If you want more love in your life, be love. If you want more abundance, find within you the abundance of your soul. If you want more joy and blessings, become the radio station that is tuned to this delicious, energetic force of true ease. What we're craving is never outside of us. What we're longing for is the fullness of our own life force. When we find a way to truly be present in our highest consciousness, then we find the wholeness within. The more we broadcast this kind of frequency, the more we manifest so much around us. We are creators—we came into the world to create more love and connection and beauty. We can't create from lack; we create from a place of feeling whole.

SET YOUR RADIO DIAL

You might be wondering who the heck am I, Cathy Heller, to be asking you to make such bold shifts in the way you think about wealth, success, and life itself. Why have I written a whole book about this? I'll tell you—I've been on a quest for over three decades. My parents had a hard marriage and a horrible divorce. I went through a lot of painful times, and I saw my mother struggle with intense heartache, depression, and anxiety. My dad left when I was a tween and things were extremely difficult. I felt very lost and broken. At age fifteen I started seeking answers and looking for the meaning of life. I wound up spending three years studying in Jerusalem, followed by learning meditation and mindfulness at UCLA. Eventually I started teaching meditation and then began coaching thousands of women, leading retreats, and teaching courses. I built a multimillion-dollar business by following my passion. In 2017, I started a podcast that allowed me to interview more than nine hundred brilliant minds including Deepak Chopra, Jon Kabbat Zinn, Byron Katie, Mitch Albom, and Marianne Williamson, to name a few. I learned that you don't have to live a life of quiet desperation or buy into hustle culture to be fulfilled; rather, there is a path to abundance and happiness that is paved with ease. The beautiful thing about truth is that all rivers lead to the same ocean. Everyone winds up at the same destination, and that journey is what I want to continue sharing with you in this book.

PLUG IN

Whenever I talk in my coaching or workshops about money, abundance, and the things we most desire in our lives, there's an impatience that will swell in the room until finally someone asks—

But what's the actionable strategy?

How do I actually do it?

The answer: Create a ripple effect with your energy.

Like skipping stones in a pond, our energy makes an impression, and it casts ripples into the universe. In its simplest form, the world is energy— made from energy, a creator and radiator of energy, dictated by energy. *You*, too, are made of energy, and so the actionable strategy for tapping into the infinite stream of abundance has everything to do with *you*.

What are you broadcasting?

What is the vibrational imprint you are leaving on the world?

What frequency are you tuned into?

Harnessing and being intentional with your energy *is* the actionable strategy.

It's not about what you do.
It's about who you are.

Your biggest gift to the world is your presence, your pure energy. Think about it—one of the highest compliments to receive is "You've got great energy." Right? Sure, it feels good to have someone compliment your hair, your smile, the college you went to, the work you do, but when someone notices your energy, that's above and beyond. When you are a walking, talking vibration of pure energy, there's nothing more attractive, more delicious.

Tuning into your unique energy isn't only liberating; it also catapults your ability to manifest. Here's a fun example from Matthew McConaughey's story that he shared when he was on my podcast.

Before he became known as the hot guy on our movie screens, he'd been going to law school until he realized he actually didn't want to be a lawyer. He summoned the courage to face his very tough Texan dad: "I can't do this anymore. I'm dropping out of law school. I don't want to be a lawyer. I actually want to be an actor." He recalled that he was so scared to do this, and cringed, wondering, *What's he going to say?*

His dad's response was, "Well, don't half-ass it." Matthew thought, *All right, I can live with that.*

He was feeling so good because he broke through the limiting garbage that allowed him to fully make the decision to become an actor. As the story goes, he went with his girlfriend to the bar at the Hyatt Hotel. They were having free drinks because his friend from film school was the bartender, and as they were enjoying free vodka tonics, his bartender friend said, "Hey, there's a guy in the bar who's in town producing a film. Let me introduce you to him. His name's Don Phillips." Four hours later and a few more vodka tonics deep, Don Phillips and Matthew got kicked out of the bar for being too loud and obnoxious. Don offered to drop Matthew off at home, and on the drive back, Don asked him, "Hey, have you ever done any acting? There's this script called *Dazed and Confused*, a movie I'm in town producing. You might be right for this small part. Come to this address tomorrow morning, and I'll have the scenes written for you."

Matthew picked up the script the next day and saw there was a handwritten note from Don with three scenes marked. He worked on the three scenes for two weeks, came back and read for the part, and got it.

On his first day of shooting, Matthew walked onto the set and the director, Richard Linklater, took a break in the middle of shooting, came over, and looked him up and down. Then the director said, "Hang on a second. You see that woman right there? She's one of the characters in the movie. Would you ask her out?"

Matthew said, "Yeah, I would definitely ask her out."

The director said, "Cool. Can you pick her up in a scene?"

Matthew took thirty minutes to figure out what he was going to say. There wasn't anything written for him, and now he'd been asked to improvise the scene.

They put a mic on him and got him in the car, and he was about to shoot his first scene in the first movie he'd ever shot without a word of dialogue having been written.

All of a sudden he heard, "Action!"

He put the car in drive, and the next words that came out of his mouth were "All right. All right. All right." Those were the very first words he ever said on film. And the rest is history.

I love this story because it's an example of the synchronicity that meets us when we are truly in alignment with our authentic self. It's an important reminder that there's so much magic that we can create when we tune into our own music, our own vibration. Our energy becomes a match for miracles.

Instead of asking yourself
What am I supposed to do?, **ask yourself**
Who am I supposed to be?

PLUGGING IN

The most impactful people in the world of tech, fashion, business, and music are tuned into the frequency of abundance. Their creative energy ripples outward, touching everyone in their orbit, making an imprint on the world.

We all know people who emit palpable, positive energy, and these are the folks we all ought to emulate. I say this as if it's that simple. And while it *is* simple, that doesn't make it necessarily easy. Often people attend my live workshops or leave a note in the chat on Zoom and ask, "But, how? How do I make it happen? What's the actionable strategy?"—I understand and empathize with their frustration. Most of us are focused on the physical world and on taking physical action, and what I suggest is counterintuitive, so allow me to make the point another way.

My husband, Lowell, is a lawyer by trade and a practical man who thinks decisions through *very carefully.* I'm more spontaneous. I tend to act before I think. When we moved into our current house, we made a list of new things we needed and others we wanted to replace. Without consulting my husband, I went on a spending spree on Amazon, and when I was finished, there was only one item left on our list that we needed: a toaster. He appealed to me, "You bought everything else. Let this be one thing that I get to buy."

A solid point and a fair request.

"Go for it," I said, and thought, *How hard could it be?* We drive past Home Goods and Target every day on the way to the girls' school. Amazon Prime delivers while we sleep. And still, it was six weeks before I could toast my bagel. When the toaster finally did arrive, Lowell's argument was that he wanted to be sure to buy the one with the best reviews, and that took time to research.

Okay, I thought, *let the man have his fancy toaster.*

The first morning that I went to use our shiny new toaster, I couldn't figure it out. This toaster had so many settings, so many bells and whistles, I thought I might need to watch a YouTube tutorial to figure it out. Finally, in frustration, I called out to Lowell: "It's not working!" A minute later, my husband calmly walked into the kitchen, assessed the situation, and, with a smile, reached behind the appliance and held up the cord. "Cath, you have to plug it in."

I felt like an idiot, but I loved the metaphor. An expensive, beautiful toaster is useless if it's not plugged in. And similarly, we don't perform at optimal efficiency if we don't plug into our own life force. It is that simple—you must plug yourself into the energetic current of life before anything good can happen.

THE WRONG OUTLET

The number-one reason why we're not plugged in, feeling toasty on the inside and emanating our magnetic life force outward, is that we've been thrown off track, believing that we must plug into external sources to turn on the heat. We've been taught to believe that our fortune and fulfillment will be found by plugging into the right relationship, the right job, the right house, the right vacation. Our culture encourages us to plug into our phones and other devices to fill us up. We've been taught to outsource our lives, when the opposite is true. The only outlet that truly works is the one located within. And if you believe this isn't true, if you believe that you possess only lack, limitation, and emptiness inside, then you don't know of what you're truly made.

YOU ARE SAFE to be abundant because the universe is abundant, powerful, and safe. It's a force. And from this place of higher consciousness, you are available to repair, to create, to flow like a river. What allows you to do that, and what allows you to be authentic, is that you are protected on the highest level by your consciousness, the part of you that's connected to divinity. The part of you that is the most relaxed is the most powerful part; it protects you and gives you your capacity to create, to say what you mean to do. You are safe when you come from that consciousness.

If you believe that you possess only lack, limitation, and emptiness inside, then you don't know of what you're truly made.

MEDITATION: MY LIGHTNESS OF BEING

The purpose of this meditation is to align your energy with the infinite stream of abundance.

Breathe in: I am not my thoughts.
Breathe out: My true self is the lightness of being that's beyond the narrative of my mind.
Breathe in: I am not my ego. I am not separate and alone.
Breathe out: I am infinite.
Breathe in: I am light, bright, limitless love.
Breathe out: My essence is whole. There's *nothing* to wish for; it's already within.

As you continue to breathe, notice the part of you that is an endless flow of energy, connected to the symphony of the universe. Feel into that vibration and listen closely. Can you hear the melody of wholeness?

Asking for an abundant life is not selfish or shameful, something to feel guilty or embarrassed about. Abundance is your inherent right. It's within; it's the current of life. Think about a redwood tree: it wants to grow tall, and the eagle above it wants to soar. Everything in this natural world is here to thrive, including you. We are each made to grow, to soar, to thrive, and when we don't, when we feel in lack it's because we're out of alignment with our soul's intention. We're not plugged in.

Plug in now.

And when you're fully charged, you become magnetic. People can't wait to work with you or be in a relationship with you because you've become an energetic match for receiving infinite abundance. In terms of receiving material wealth, it's always our energy that opens that lock. Holding a positive vibration is what turns the key.

Our feelings of lack and separation are generated by the mind. But you are not your thoughts; you're not the voices in your head. Rather, you are an extension of the infinite, endless light that is, was, and always will be. The more we can quiet the swirling mind, the more we can connect with our source of abundance, the one hidden in plain sight. This is why meditation and bringing your attention to the present moment is so important because everything we're seeking is already here within us. So many of us have bought into the illusion of separation: "what's theirs is theirs and what's mine is mine." On a physical, 3-D level, we "see" a world of separation. Yet what I have come to understand is that on an energetic level, all that exists is Oneness. If only we could fashion glasses that allowed us to see beyond 3-D. What would we see? Ribbons of energy within one infinite field. Sound waves wrapping around Earth like a rainbow. If we could see beyond 3-D, we'd instantly recognize that we're all connected to one another by the lightness of our own being, as each wave and ripple is connected by the wholeness of the ocean.

SOMETIMES PEOPLE WONDER if it's a contradiction to be deeply spiritual and wealthy at the same time. Somehow there is this false belief that the more spiritual a person is the less they should have. My friend Emily

Fletcher asked me, "How did you go from studying in Jerusalem to teaching people how to manifest millions of dollars?"

My answer: "Because they're totally the same."

"Say more!" she insisted.

So here is what I shared.

I have come to understand, it turns out, that our whole job here is to have radical reception and to be receivers, period. To move out of our resistant thoughts and into an elevated vibration where we are receptive and operating in a flow state. The ego-mind thinks it's separate from all other things in this world, that it's bad when one individual receives more because that means there is less for you and for everyone else. But if we're all One and each of us is part of the Oneness, why wouldn't you want everyone to receive? Each of us is receiving on behalf of the collective. You would never look at that redwood tree and think it should have only a small amount of water or worry that it's too tall. You don't judge the redwood tree for taking up too much space, because if you zoom out, a redwood tree is adding to the total health and magnificence of the whole forest.

The ego would have us believe that it's separate from all other things in this world, and that is why the assignment for each of us is to live life from a higher place of consciousness and set down the ego. We're all here to thrive and expand our capacity to receive on behalf of the whole. We must learn to reject scarcity consciousness, which makes us feel that others having more means that there is not enough for us. Thinking that way is in opposition to abundance. And it is now the way the universe is made.

THE PROBLEM WITH PROBABILITY

Do you often make decisions about the present and future based on the past? This is how most people live. They perceive their reality from a place of probability. They're thinking about what's probable and that's as far as they can see.

So there's probability or there's possibility. Let that sink in.

When we hyperfocus on the "how," we become stuck in the realm of probability. And one of the biggest problems with probability is that it nudges us to look for evidence in the past, to look for predictable patterns and outcomes *from before* that will inform how things unfold in the future. And where there is a reasonable argument to be made that the past can and does often inform the future, probability inhibits possibility.

Other people are making decisions based on possibility, which means they're not living from the past. They're living from possibility, which is endless. They're open to all potentials and all potentials always exist. The people who I've interviewed on my podcast, the greatest minds, the greatest creative geniuses, do not live in a state of probability. They're all possibilities. They're constantly seeing further. They're constantly seeing what's beyond what's already been done.

Probability inhibits possibility.

So often we get stuck in the same little loop because, even though there is a bigger arena to play in, we don't see it. And if *you* don't see it, it doesn't exist for you. Probability keeps us confined to a 3-D world, while abundance flows outside those boundaries, and your ability to access richness, in all its interpretations and forms, requires you to shift your focus from the analytical to the magical realm of possibility. Full stop. And when you do that, you will inevitably start to see what you didn't see before. The movie of your life will shift from black and white to Technicolor, like when Dorothy walks out of her Kansas house into the Land of Oz. And as you move forward on your own yellow brick road, you'll feel yourself lining up with possibility. You'll feel yourself align with a new truth: all potentials exist. And what happened *before* won't necessarily predict *what comes next*. Click your heels and repeat after me: I want to go home to infinite possibility.

Nearly every inspirational person I've had on my podcast followed possibility. They didn't arrive where they are because they took the road most probable. When I interviewed Alex Banayan, who wrote *The Third Door: The Wild Quest to Uncover How the World's Most Successful People Launched Their Careers*, he explained his "why" behind speaking with successful individuals like Warren Buffett, Bill Gates, Maya Angelou, Lady Gaga, and Steven Spielberg—he wanted to understand how they arrived at this point in their lives, and he began explaining success as a series of doors. Most people, he explained, wait for the first door. They are waiting to get in at the nightclub or the restaurant or the lecture hall, and there's a line to get through the door, and most people will wait their whole lives to go through that door. Next, there is the second door reserved for people with privilege and power and status. These are the "gold status" members of the general public, and this line is shorter yet harder to get through. Finally, there is a third door that has no line at all and which you can walk straight through, but the trick about this door is finding it. It's not clearly marked; however, it is there, and this is the door that folks like Warren Buffett, Bill Gates, Maya Angelou, Lady Gaga, and Steven Spielberg walked through. What Banayan discovered was that the most successful people were the ones who had the courage to step out of line for Door Number One and look for the unmarked door that led directly to where they wanted to go.

Most of us are in line. We believe that we must wait for whatever comes next, and sometimes, we convince ourselves that we must wait a very long time, and even then, we may not reach the front of the line. It takes courage to get out of line, then, and lose our spot, but if we never look for the unmarked door, we have no hope of finding it. Door Number Three presents our greatest challenge and reward, so ask yourself: Can you get out of the line of probability and go through the door of possibility?

When it comes to abundance, there's nothing wrong with having money. Why? Because you came to be a steward of all energy. You came to be a steward of love. You came to be a steward of abundance, compassion, and creativity, and money is among the resources that allows us to generate and maximize how we can impact and transform our lives and the larger world. Why would you limit that?

CHANGE THE DIAL FROM PROBABILITY TO POSSIBILITY

Take a few minutes and think about the vision, the dream you have for yourself. Allow it to arrive in your mind in its brightest, *biggest* technicolor splendor. Got it captured in your mind? Okay, now, I want you to finish the following two prompts:

My brightest, *biggest* technicolor vision of my life includes the following five details. (Include things like location—where you live and travel—your profession and play activities—what you do for paid and unpaid work—the people around you, the dollar amount in your bank account, the state of your health, how you feel when you wake up in the morning, and so on.)

_____

_____

_____

_____

_____

_____

_____

Once you have some of the biggest, brightest details of your vision documented above, I want you to finish the next prompt.

When I think about the vision I have for myself and my life, it will *probably* end up looking closer to this:

_____

_____

_____

_____

_____

_____

_____

In the chapters ahead, we're going to have you step into your true identity, which is beyond the body, time, and space—it's pure energy. The true and essential "you" has never changed. And the same thread that runs through Michael Jordan and Oprah and Beyoncé and Picasso runs through you. Energy. Unfortunately, most people never tap into their own energy reserves. It's like giving someone a Tesla and all they're thinking about is how to turn it on and drive to the grocery store. But it's not built to do that. It has so many other powerful functions. There is so much *more* when we tap into our energy flow.

If you want to live a more abundant life, there's one thing you can do—and it is to make yourself flow ready. When you're in flow, you're free of self-consciousness. You've let go of the self. And what happens when you drop the ego self, something bigger than you are moves through you, and it feels like you're floating because you are not controlling it. It is moving through you. When you're in flow state, it's a "yes and," which is one of the basic rules of improv. Whatever someone throws at you, you work with it. You say "yes and," and then whatever the universe throws at you, you say, "Yes, and let's go." That is literally the Jedi mind trick. If you study any kind of energy work, whether it's Tai Chi or any of those elements, they're moving from using what's there and then moving it somewhere else. Resistance hasn't ever gotten anyone anywhere. It's about "yes and."

You want to live up to your potential. You want to be abundant. You want to have access to your most abundant life. So what needs to happen? You must set down the old predictable probable identity and start playing with the Tesla that you are and start utilizing all its functions. If you're saying to yourself, *Well, I don't have that capacity. Only Michelangelo has that*—that's just not true. Every single one of us has the same inherent capacity to move into flow, where all potential exists. It's all here. It's all available.

What's happening, though, is there's a limit on how much you can receive because you're not tapped into who you really are and what's really possible. The small self can become scared to let go, scared for you to receive. It can get scared for you to have these bigger, more flowy kinds of experiences. So, you need to remember who you are. Because you're pretending anyway; you're pretending to be somebody who is not available and is obsessed with what's predictable. But that's not really you. You're here for a mystical experience. You're here for an abundant experience, which means you're going to have to stop playing from that place.

The more that you start to perceive yourself as abundant, the more you move into flow. You move into ultimate creativity, and you'll just notice that everything starts to line up in your life. And there's a synchronicity that meets you there when you're playing with this beautiful energy of this universe and you're ready for it and you're allowing it in and then you start to see all potentials exist. It's the best feeling in the world. And in that flow, you're going to start to have tiny whispers that you don't yet perceive. Those whispers will get stronger, and then your life will become more clear. And then you'll make a move.

WEALTHY AF

When I ask women to declare that they want to be healthy, they are inspired and ready to tell the world. They feel excited to prioritize their physical fitness and even hopeful to influence others to do the same. However, when I ask women to say "I want to be wealthy AF," they're met with so much resistance. What does that statement bring up for you when you say it out loud? Does it feel attainable? Does it make you feel nervous or scared? Notice how you feel because if you perceive that something is dangerous or uncomfortable, you will protect yourself from allowing it in. You'll just spin around and around thinking it feels impossible.

When we talk about who we really are in our essence—not the personality—we enter a superconscious mode beyond the small self and into the big Self. The big Self exists beyond time, beyond space, beyond the predictable, and in this space there's no resistance. In this space, you're available for an abundance of energy because it's moving through you like a lightning rod.

The whole idea is being who you truly are, which is this bold, beautiful, brilliant, energetic resource that transmits energy to the entire ecosystem. That's your job: to transmit.

MOVE WITH THE CURRENT

Money comes from the word *currency*. Currency comes from the word *current*. It's got to keep moving. It's not supposed to stay with you. It's supposed to move through you. And so this is the problem: ego-minded, fear-based thought doesn't understand what money is and it's about holding onto it. But that's not the job of it. That's not what it's supposed to do. It's supposed to just keep moving like blood moves through the body. It can't stop. If it stops, we've got a blood clot. We've got a problem. It's got to keep moving, right? Think about water. Water has got to move. If it doesn't move, what happens? It becomes poison. It can kill you. But if it's moving, you can drink it. It's clean. Same thing with money. It's got to move. As soon as it comes in, you should know where it's going out. What are you doing with it? Don't hold it. It's not there to be held. You've got to put it back into the market. What does that do? It builds more wealth. You could invest it or hire someone and do lots of good things with it.

This is the paradigm shift. You're going to allow yourself to generate more money because it's not about you. It's about us. It's not about you and me being separate. It's about us. Can you be in stewardship of it? Can you be in contribution? Can you be in fullness? Yes. That's actually your job.

When I think of money, I think of it the same way as I think about the universe—it is a constant, abundant, expansive force of possibility. It's unbounded energy, and the more energy that I can bring through me, it's like I'm just moving things in a five-dimensional space. Money is one of those things. How much more of that can come in and then create more possibility? How much more love can come in? How many more ideas can I create? And it's all part of the same soup for me. It's not separate. It's all tied together.

The more we're a vessel to receive, the more we know we're in flow, the more we know we're connected to the divine. It's such a change from the way you've been taught. When you move on from that, you won't believe how available your vibration is for it. Then the opportunities come in, then you're okay with playing with it. You're okay with charging more. You're okay with walking around and knowing that you are worth more because you're a custodian for wealth. That's the current. That's the currency. You have the capacity to move it. How much power do you have to let it in and move it through you? You're going to start to see new possibilities. You're going to start to feel safe taking that next step and you're going to actually see it, whereas before, if you don't feel safe and your energy is dulled because of it, you won't even perceive the thought of it. You will be amazed. You're going to think, *She's right. Out of the blue, I could see what was already there. And I made this call. I made this move. I spoke in this way. Somebody perceived me differently. I was offered this. I was available for it.* And now you're in flow.

SO, AGAIN, the answer to the questions "How do I make more money? How do I manifest wealth? How do I move the needle?" is to plug into your own power source that is connected to the symphony of the universe and then broadcast it outwardly. And not quietly, but BIG, BOLD, LOUD, and BRIGHT. When you start to create abundance that originates within you, guess what happens next? You become a magnet for receiving *more* synchronicities and opportunities, and you create a wave of abundance for others, because when one part of the ecosystem thrives, it ripples outward. We must each trust that we are connected, that we are an extension of the infinite, and that receiving abundance is our birthright. We each must love ourselves enough to let go of our fear and control. We each must decide to let go of probability and predictability that was informed by the past. And from that place, we can plug into our magnetic life force and move into the future where all things are possible.

Here's an exercise that helps you change your state of being. You can try this out:

Close your eyes. Welcome yourself back.

Notice anything that has been making your mind busy or nervous or overwhelmed.

Just notice that. And take a deep breath. Put your hand on your belly so you can feel yourself breathe.

Let's be reminded that there is peace available and that it is safe to feel safe.

Take a deep breath again.

As you start to surrender the mind, your soul is welcoming you home. And you're so happy to be back in the centered place where there's nothing urgent. Do you feel connected to the stars, to the earth, to all the beings, to God as part of you that is connected to the infinite quantum field? Because the field is energy, and you are made of energy. And just as you become aware and you put your attention there, your resonance starts to ripple in a greater way.

Feel the tuning fork that is your energetic signature. See if you can notice from the top of your head this life force coming in the source of this frequency.

With every breath, allow this tuning fork to offer a clear stronger signal, like you are the sound bowl itself and your job is to put forth a more resonant sound.

All the answers are here. You can't even put words to them; you just know them.

Picture that your energy is like a magic marker and with its vibration, it can draw your life. And the cleaner and more receptive the vibration, the more beautiful the world it creates.

Now, as if you were watching a stop-motion movie, just picture this vibration drawing your vision into life.

What do you start to see come into focus?

For the part of your mind that wants to know what it needs to do, let the wisdom within you tell you what you need to do for this to come to be. Because the mind wants a job. What is your being? What is your self? What do you need to do to co-create this?

When you're ready, open your eyes.

2.

CONNECTING TO THE DIVINE

HOW A DAY OF FRUSTRATION
BECAME A BLESSING

When I was nineteen, my sister told me that she was flying down from New York to go to Orlando on a Shabbaton. I didn't know what that word meant, *Shabbaton*. I wasn't spiritual at all then and I seriously thought she'd joined a cult. I was attending Florida State University at the time and we didn't see each other that often, so I said, "All right, I'll drive the three and a half hours, and I'll meet you there." She said, "Great! Why don't you come on Sunday morning after the event?" That was the plan.

Keep in mind this was before cell phones, around 2001. I had to call my answering machine to get her voice message with the address and print out the directions from MapQuest.com. It was a retreat site in the middle of nowhere in Orlando, so I was having trouble finding it. All I knew was that she told me to get there by ten in the morning because she was leaving for the airport at noon.

As I was driving, I got more and more lost. And then I started thinking, *This is insane. I've now driven for three and a half hours and I'm still not there. I don't know where I am. Why am I continuing to drive? Because she's gonna leave for the airport at noon, and at this rate, I'm going to miss her.* We were only going to have two hours together.

Sure enough, I got there at, like, 12:15 p.m. No one was there. I parked the car and got out. There was a volleyball net and some beautiful trees, but no one was in sight. I was so frustrated that I'd just driven all the way down and would have to drive another three and a half hours home feeling so unsatisfied. It was such a waste of a day, and I didn't even get to see my sister.

Then about one hundred yards away, I saw a figure walking toward me. I didn't know who it was. I heard him say, "Hey, are you Barbara's sister?" It was like something out of a movie. He was walking out of the fog, holding a basketball. He said, "This is crazy. I'm so tired. I was up all night talking to different people. I was about to take a nap. And something told me to get up, walk outside. And here you are. Your sister told me last night, 'You have to meet my sister. I wish my sister was here.' So, I think that you and I are supposed to meet."

I started crying, partly because I was still frustrated, but also because when someone is that kind to you, you can't help but tear up a little more. He looked at me and said, "Wow. That's amazing. You're seeing the situation one way, and I see it totally differently." He said, "This wasn't about your sister. What if this is about *us*? What if we're supposed to meet? I think you and I are supposed to have a conversation."

He then said, "Okay, let's start with the most important question."

I said, "What is it?"

"You like tuna fish?"

"All right, sure."

"Great, I think there's still food in the kitchen. Let's go have lunch."

CONNECTING TO THE DIVINE

We sat down for lunch and wound up talking until almost seven o'clock at night.

As I was getting ready to leave, he said, "Do you want to come back on Thursday and spend Shabbat with us before I head back to Israel?"

I had no idea what was happening, but something in me told me to say yes. So, I came back on Thursday, thanks to this invitation from my new friend Rabbi Binny Freedman.

I was graduating from college a few months later when he called me. "Hey, do you want to come to Jerusalem and learn?"

I said, "Yes, that would be amazing."

That began my journey to Israel, where a three-week trip turned into a nearly three-year spiritual immersion. And that experience led me to this work and this book that you're reading today.

This was one of those life moments when you think things are going so wrong, but God is at work, moving you to where you actually need to be.

After I graduated from college in 2001, I traveled to Jerusalem for what was meant to be a short vacation. I figured I would go experience the Holy Land and then apply to graduate school in New York. I wasn't feeling sure about what my next step in life was. Many of my friends were going to law school or starting their careers. I had a desire to explore the world. I was thirsty for a mystical experience of my own. On the day I was initially meant to leave for the airport, a friend of mine invited me to a class and I learned my first piece of Jewish wisdom, which completely changed my life.

The class was taught by a man named Rabbi David Zeller (who has since passed away, may his memory be a blessing). He was a psychologist who had also been a Buddhist and he had returned to his Jewish roots. He had a sweet smile and a scruffy beard and wore Birkenstock sandals. His energy was loving and pure.

He explained that we learn the meaning of Hebrew words from the very first time that we see the word used in the Torah (the Old Testament). He wrote the Hebrew word *Shabbat* on the board, which is the sabbath. He said the first time this word is used is when Abraham is sitting at the foot of the tent, meditating. He said, "The word Shabbat/the sabbath means to meditate." He went on to say that as Abraham sat in stillness, eventually God appeared to him. He said that connection is available to all of us.

What I learned that day is that as soon as we stop doing and sit in our own stillness, God appears, because we connect with that elevated state of consciousness, the part of us that is our true Self. That part of us is connected to the infinite stream. Just like God created the world and rested on the seventh day, we all need time to reconnect so that we can hear the divine within us. The word for God in Hebrew is a word that means *is, was, and will be.* God in the Jewish lens is the energy of infinite intelligence, the source of all life, the creative force that is beyond time, beyond space, connecting everything. It is the energy that can't be created or destroyed, that gives life to and unites everything. It is beyond what we can comprehend because it is infinite in nature and not meant for us to fully grasp with our minds.

I decided right then and there to extend my trip, and later that evening went to my first Shabbat dinner in Jerusalem.

Even though I am Jewish, I hadn't really ever experienced Shabbat. I wasn't raised with traditions or any kind of religious education; in fact, my understanding of Judaism didn't extend much beyond Jerry Seinfeld, the Holocaust, Mel Brooks, and Sunday morning bagels with lox and cream cheese. That was my truth at the time, and I was interested in learning more, so I accepted the Shabbat dinner invitation and found myself—for the first time in my life—experiencing the most love I had ever felt.

It was at this dinner where I met my dear teacher Rabbi Aaron. He was hosting the evening in the Old City of Jerusalem, and the small room was filled with candles. Once everyone arrived, he invited us to light an individual candle and as we did, he said, "Most of you do not know each other, but you've come together tonight and when we look at our collective candle-light, we feel we are no longer strangers because we are one. This feeling of connection and oneness is what we're always seeking. This is the meaning of bliss." His words stunned me, and I began to cry because what he was describing was something I'd longed for my whole life but hadn't believed was possible. And if it was, I didn't know how to access it. Suddenly, a new possibility had presented itself and I was so grateful to have canceled my flight back home and I decided I would stay for as long as time allowed. I dedicated myself to learning all that I could about Jewish mysticism and ultimately how to find deeper purpose in life.

Shabbat was a game changer for me. I regarded it as an invitation to connect with my soul and to spend a day with other people where I was no longer trying to build the world into something new; rather, I was appreciating everything for what it already is. For twenty-four hours, I didn't need to fix or change anything; rather, I needed to be with things exactly as they are. There is an equanimity and peace in that day of meditation. I started keeping Shabbat in my early twenties. That one day out of the week, I would pause and enjoy being free of my cell phone. For one day I wasn't a human doing; I was a human being.

What I learned in Israel taught me how to change my own radio dial from feeling empty, disconnected, sad, and unworthy to feeling connected, full, and at peace. I realized that the most powerful resource was love and that each of us had an abundance of love because at our core we were love itself. The mystic was within us. We held the power all along. The more we tuned into the wholeness within, the more we manifested wholeness all around us.

You see, despite what you may have believed all along, abundance isn't made of material things. It's a state of being that you can access, and when you connect to this elevated state, you can go from living in despair to feeling joy and love, moved by the music of life.

This idea of Oneness is so central to the way Einstein talks about the universe and the unified field, but Abraham was the first person to say that God is this Oneness. Abraham had a radically different perception of God being this source of energy that is, was, and always will be.

The central prayer in Judaism is *Shema' Yisrael Hashem Elokeinu Hashem Echad*, which means essentially *God is One*. But what does that really mean? It means that everything is within this One and that the divine is the source of all that is, and since it's infinite, it's also within and beyond all that is. If God is infinite, then there isn't anywhere God isn't. It means the whole world is made of atoms and it's all energy swirling, in the same way that every single wave is part of the ocean. Rabbi Aaron taught me that we are each a masterpiece, a piece of the master. If God were the sun, we would each be a ray of her light. Everyone embodies a unique aspect of the ecosystem; like the different instruments that form one orchestra, we each are born to play a unique part and together it makes a symphony.

A FEW DAYS BEFORE I was supposed to leave Israel, I wandered into a local clothing shop. It was customary for women in the Old City to wear skirts, but for my return to the States, I thought I should return in denim, so I bought myself a pair of jeans. The brand was one I hadn't seen before—True Religion—and I smiled at the symbolism. This is exactly what I'd received throughout my time in Israel—true belonging, true connection. Pure love.

I love that one of the central ideas in Judaism is that every person is intrinsically whole and connected to the infinite field. The Jewish lens doesn't believe that in order for you to be righteous, you need to be Jewish. This is why Jews don't convert people to Judaism. Most people don't realize that there are only 15 million Jews in the world. If we are all One, then we don't need to be the same. Oneness isn't sameness. Oneness means each thread in the tapestry may be a different color and it's all part of expressing the greater whole. Oneness means I love you because we're one no matter what; we don't have to be the same.

MY TIME IN JERUSALEM was a complete paradigm shift. It helped heal my broken heart, and I finally saw the world, not through limitation but through love and infinite possibility.

My past hadn't changed, my circumstances remained intact, but my internal frequency shifted from one side of the dial to the other side. And from there, my entire life changed. After I returned from Israel, doors opened, opportunities flooded in with grace and ease, and I went from having nothing in my bank account to growing a business that has generated more wealth than I ever imagined possible. I married my neighbor—literally, the boy next door—and he's a kind, loyal, and gentle man. I have three daughters, and we live in a gorgeous home overlooking the hills of Los Angeles. I have Persian kittens running around my house, many good friends, and even though I've made my professional life a priority, I never miss a school event for my three girls. I'm able to do this because my job doesn't feel like work. It doesn't feel hard or desperate. Rather, my days feel expansive and rewarding.

Change the dial,
change your life.

I want to share the principles and tools that will allow you to control your own radio dial, remove any static you hear, and tune to the channel of possibility and inner peace, to the channel of abundance. What's your deepest desire—the partner of your dreams, a fulfilling job, the security of a new home, a healthier relationship with your body, a positive relationship with money? How about more connections and deeper friendships? Release from self-doubt and pain and an uptick in healing and joy? The opportunities are endless depending on where you choose to tune your dial.

Here's what I know to be true: we're all built to receive. It's just that most of us haven't been taught how to use our apparatus, our Sony rabbit ears, and so we've come to believe that our options are limited, like having only five songs on your playlist that you listen to on repeat. Not only is this false—there are an infinite number of songs—but also, *you* are your own DJ. You dictate what music is played. You set the tone, you create the environment, so what's it going to be—a dance party or radio static? I don't know about you, but my vote is for the dance party. Name the date and time and I'm there!

**You get to have a life
that takes your breath away.**

3.

DREAM A BIGGER DREAM

L AST SUMMER, I took my kids to the National History Museum across from New York City's Central Park. After walking the equivalent of three miles, my kids started complaining about sore feet, so we decided to take in a show at the planetarium. We bought tickets to the IMAX theater with surround sound, and as we sank into the comfy seats to watch a film on the solar system, I thought, *There's nothing better to open your mind.* I sat there in the dark holding my daughters' hands, looking at the moons of Pluto and Uranus and Neptune, the rings of Saturn and Jupiter spinning in magical coherence and the cosmic dance of our solar system. Tears began streaming down my face and Lowell leaned over and whispered in my ear, "Are you okay?" "Yes." I smiled. "It's so beautiful to be part of something so vast, so beautifully limitless and majestic."

**The universe is a perfect
orchestration of abundance.**

This universe, this *actual* universe we're living in, goes on and on. It's unbelievably expansive. Beautiful. And infinite. That *is* reality, and it is *our* reality. And yet, how many times a day do you run into someone who says, "You know, the reality is . . ." and they finish the sentence with a limiting belief, like "the reality is there's just not enough money, energy, time, resources, talent, people, interest, buy-in, space, demand in my dream to make it happen"?

Don't make limitation your reality.

Your capacity to experience the fullness, expansiveness, and abundance of life is calling out to you. Do you hear it? It's an enchanting whisper. You are here, on Earth, within this solar system, to experience all the wonderment and generosity of the universe. You are limited only by your own limitation.

TAKING OFF THE SOMEBODY SUIT

When we are so bought into our somebody suit, as Ram Dass calls it, then unfortunately we play by the rules of space and time. But everything that's ever been created is beyond space and time. DNA created all of us faster than space and time. In fact, it was created in an energy bang. Literally. That code of energy created the 3-D printout that is each of us. So, the more you move into consciousness and loosen the grip on the somebody that you think you are, and you move more into nobody, nowhere, no time, just your essence, your essential self, your soul, you're a much better creator in that place. That's where all potentials exist. That's where things get made. And it might take a minute for you to see all the potential that surrounds you because the speed of light is slower than consciousness. Outside the solar system, time evaporates. That's how fast it moves. There is no time.

Let me walk you through this. Here on Earth, a day is 24 hours. A day on Jupiter is about 9 hours and 56 minutes. So why is a day 9 hours and 56 minutes on Jupiter and 24 hours here? Because of the planets' rotational speeds in relationship to the sun. The only reason we have a 24-hour day is because of Earth's rotational speed. What happens when you go to Pluto? A day is 153 hours. And what happens when you measure time somewhere in the universe where there isn't any light? Time doesn't exist. Time evaporates completely.

We think that our solar system is all there is. But the universe is vast and our solar system is like a dot. This means most of the universe has no time. Why is this? The speed of light is the fastest thing that we can calculate and measure—it's the only dimension we can see with our naked eye. When you close your eyes, you go into quantum time. You can perceive a lot more potential—actually, you can perceive an infinite amount. When you're in quantum time and you hit a peak state of meditation, if you had a scan of your brain waves you'd see they go to gamma. Gamma waves are thought to be faster than the speed of light. That's where things are created. Things are not created on a three-dimensional level. That's just the printout that took a delay for you to finally see it. That's why I love teaching meditation, because your creations have to happen in that dimension. They're not going to happen when you perceive at the speed of light. That's the slow-motion version. That's only showing you the past. Anything that you're seeing in 3-D, it happened before. You created that with a consciousness from the past.

Usually, the list of things on your want list are not even close to what you actually could create. So often in my workshops, people's lists of things that they want reflect things they've been told to want or that they think they should want. Sometimes it's because other people seem to feel so great, their lives look so good to us, that we think we'll feel just as good if we can have what they have. But what I have learned is that striving for what others have is never going to lead to true abundance. I want to teach you how to tune into yourself and how to create a wish list based on your own true frequency. Because when you start to listen, you will find that you've actually got a better idea for your wish list. You just don't even know what that looks like yet, but the more you hang out in a higher state of consciousness, you'll be surprised and think, *Whoa, I can't believe that just happened. That was even better than the thing I wanted to happen.*

When we want to create, we must drop the ego. We must drop the expectations. We must drop the story. We must drop all the fear. All that stuff is happening here, but it's not where we create. Creation happens in wholeness, which happens when things are lightning fast. That's why you can move in leaps and bounds when you're aligned, because your frequency is creating at such a rapid level. And then anything that you do down there just moves time. It's unbelievable. You can skip a lot of the ineffective things that you plan to do when you go to the place where things are created. That's why most people at some point just decide, "You know what, the hell with it. I'm going to learn to meditate because I can't afford to not do that. I can't afford to not be creating in my life and creating the things that I want." Those things you want are all already there, but they happen from being in that space and therefore become a match to that vibration because you're playing in that level. And you'll start to create things that are so much bigger and better that surprise you, when you're in that place.

It is really fascinating how most of the time we are suffering unnecessarily because of misperceptions about reality. Too often, we see limitations, risks, or dangers. But there's literally a whole range of higher frequencies at which we can create. There is no need to stay stuck in this one little spot. Your best bet, then, is to pay attention to your own personal feelings of flow, fluidity, and calm. When you learn to tune into those feelings, you will begin to move toward a new vision for your life that feels genuinely, authentically incredible—on your terms, not someone else's.

LIMITED DREAMS

We've been talking about how we create our reality through our thoughts and beliefs, and now let's lean into the vision you have for yourself. The *you* of your dreams. The you who is free of living your life on other people's terms. The authentic you.

I recently posed this question to a woman in my online coaching program: "When you think of your future self, where are you sitting? What are you eating? Who are you with? What are you wearing?"

"Oh, I don't see all those details," the woman said. "I just know I want to do more to help other women. That's my dream."

"Supporting women is a wonderful goal, a beautiful vision," I said, "but let me ask you again to describe to me in detail who you are when you're living your *biggest*, most expansive life. Because I want to let you in on a little secret . . . the person with the biggest vision wins."

Crickets. She had no response. She was silent, and this is what happens over and over and over again when I talk to women about what they really want. They don't have an answer. Why? Because they won't give themselves permission to reach for it. Fear blocks our ability to see unlimited potential.

DREAMS UNLIMITED

Our universe is infinite. There are no boundaries. And yet, again, we don't experience our lives like that. So many of us live within constrictions. We draw tight perimeters around our lives when we could be living and *playing* in the entire solar system. So, I want you to take a minute now to allow yourself to dream without limitation, to believe that every potential, every possibility exists, and I want you to play out the possibility.

DROP IN

Make yourself comfortable and take some deep meditative breaths. When you feel ready, picture your life a year from now. How do you spend your days? Where are you living? With whom are you living? How are you nourishing your body on every level—spiritually, mentally, and physically? I want you to imagine the fullness of it, all the colors on the canvas. Do you have a picture in your mind? Remember that the mind loves to create limits and false beliefs around what's possible or "realistic." If you can, ask your thoughts to step to the side, and allow your vision to come forward.

Next, picture that it's five years from now, and imagine that for five full years, you've shown up for yourself in a greater way—with more intention and consciousness. In this vision, what new opportunities have presented themselves? How have you modeled for your family and friends and for other women a new possibility, of a life that feels abundant and that is within reach? If you get stuck in your head (it happens!) evaluating whether you *think* your dream is possible, or whether you *believe* you're worthy of having the life of your dreams, try it again. Take a deep breath and set your sticky resistance to the side. Give yourself permission to release any tension you're holding. Let it go, and play out the possibility again. Play it out as far as it will go. Allow yourself to enjoy this vision of yourself, living in full color like Mary Poppins when she jumps into the drawing on the sidewalk. Boom! Jump into your drawing and see where it takes you. What are you doing? Who are you with? How does it look and sound in the movie of your life? You're the director, so you can select the cast, the wardrobe and props, the scenery and script. Your imagination and the possibilities are endless. Play it out and *feel* into it.

Now imagine that it's ten years from now. What incredible experiences have you had, that you wouldn't have had if you hadn't allowed yourself to receive? In this future vision of yourself, how has your energy impacted this world? Imagine yourself in the home you're in now, and there's a knock at the door, and when you open it, there's someone standing there who puts their hand on their heart and thanks you for impacting their life. And right behind her, comes another person who says the same thing. Before you know it, your entire front yard is filled with people whose lives have been touched by you. Your neighborhood is filled with people you've not met personally but who thank you for the gifts you have given them.

Can you imagine this? Can you imagine having an impact like this? How does it feel? Allow yourself to really feel into it, and then— name the feeling. If it helps you to identify and name it, take out a sheet of paper and draw a circle that looks like the sun. In the center, write a few descriptor words to describe the dream you just imagined for yourself. It could be as simple as the words *home* or *new relationship* or *impactful career change*. Once you've written down a few words to describe your dream, draw several lines out from your sun, and on those lines, write the *feelings* that your dreams pull forward. What does it feel like to make that career change, move into a new relationship, make more money? Does it feel peaceful, nourishing, stable, abundant? Whatever the feelings, write them down and recognize that those feelings are what you're really after. The feeling that accompanies your Mary Poppins moment is what you *really* want. It's not the petticoats, or the catchy song or tap dancing with Dick Van Dyke. It's the feeling that your vision inspires. And that feeling is not external to you. It's internal and now.

Your desired feelings are always within reach. You can bring them forth like you do any other memory because the feeling you're after is one you've felt before—otherwise, you wouldn't be able to identify it and crave it. Even if only for brief periods, you have felt peace; you have felt nourished and safe. The feeling you seek is like a scene from a movie that you have unconsciously memorized. It is imprinted in the frequency of your body, which means that you can call it back. You don't have to wait to feel it again! Take a moment now and choose one of the feelings that you wrote down and then call it back by remembering a time in your life when you felt it. When you make a practice of calling forth the memory of the feeling you desire, you will attune to the frequency of your dreams and then you won't have to wait one year or five or ten to *feel* them. You'll speed up the process to meet you where you are now.

Most of us have been conditioned to think that it's more material goods that we want. This is a pervasive thought, but it doesn't make it true. It's the immaterial that we seek, the stuff that can only be found on the inside. I really began to understand this when I lived in King David's Old City in Jerusalem, where I lived like most residents in a tiny apartment filled with people and pets on a narrow, slippery street. It was crowded and yet in this dense city, the *feeling of abundance* permeates. It appears as if there is no room to move and yet there is so much space created by the current of kindness, especially on Saturdays when people celebrate the Jewish Sabbath that begins Friday afternoon and is observed until sunset the next day. I mentioned this earlier, but it is truly amazing how different an experience this was from how I was raised. A full day of rest is marked by families and friends gathering to *be*, not *do*, working *to live*, not living to work, and the feeling on this day is markedly peaceful and full of blessings. People sit together with no distractions, not rushing to be somewhere else other than at home with their families, parents putting children on their laps, holding hands and playing joyfully with their older kids. When I was young, I went to the movies and hung out in the mall with friends, but mostly by myself, buying things I didn't need. In my house, there was no connection, no togetherness, no talk of community or contribution. In Jerusalem, kindness is king. A few months into living with Rabbi Aaron and his family, I asked him, "What's the most spiritual thing I can do in Israel? Is there some place I need to go? Something specific I ought to do?" He told me there was a widow who lived a block away and that I could visit her and offer to do her dishes. "That sounds like the most spiritual thing you could do today," he said. In Israel, I experienced an abundance of love and meaning and warm chicken soup.

In contrast, I've spent many Saturdays in other places in the world where there is no rest, no sense of togetherness. Instead, there is an excess of material wealth and a poverty of the soul. What's the differentiator? In the United States, specifically, we suffer from no sense of enoughness, no rest, no pause between the notes. Our focus is on productivity, on over being, and this exacerbates a false and limiting belief that *we are not enough* whatever we have, even when we have more than most.

Now, no one is saying that you shouldn't be ambitious or that you shouldn't want material things. Personally, I love staying at beautiful resorts with gorgeous views. I love getting facials and putting amazing lotion on my hands. I love a beautiful car with a great sound system that allows me to blast my favorite music. I'll spend extra money on great seats to see my favorite artists perform live. There is nothing wrong with desiring material things and enjoying the physical offerings of this life. Understand, though, that what you're really after is the feeling, the energetic vibration that those material things inspire. For me, a beautiful resort with high-quality towels equals the feeling of ease, the feeling of being safe and pampered. A great sound system is the energetic equivalent of vitality, exhilaration, and soul expansion. And second-row tickets at the Hollywood Bowl inspire in me a feeling of connectivity, creativity, and oneness.

I want you to think about what success really looks like to you. Success to me is inner peace. No matter where I live geographically, I always live in my own inner world. I could be on the most beautiful beach in the world, but if my mind is a mess, then I'm not enjoying whatever the circumstances. Success for me is being cozy, reading a good book with my cat next to me, period. I don't have this feeling of success that's attached to a certain amount of money or followers. That would be poison for my soul. And that doesn't have to be your journey. You get to choose what success feels like. You don't have to put your ladder on anyone else's wall. Your version of success could be building a life that feels good to you. A balance where you get to make money doing things that you love and build a beautiful business that feels like alignment to you. You don't have to cosign some vision just because somebody says $10 million a year is their version of success. Check in. Does that feel like success to you? I don't know. I mean, my business doesn't make $10 million a year. There's a whole group of humans in the world who believe more is better. And it's always about more. For some it may be always about scaling and for others it may be about deepening. The success may be about arriving and enjoying the most delicious moments we can be present for, like spending time with a friend and listening to the rain.

It's always a feeling we're after— the energetic vibration of abundance.

Living an abundant life means you connect with the mystical every day. You have the freedom to live a life where limitation is replaced by expansion, where you feel ease and flow, the wind in your hair. Where you feel safe, secure, unencumbered, unleashed, to feel like your life has significance and meaning, and that *you* and what you do are valuable to the world. Me, you, all of us here on the planet—we didn't come for piles of stuff. So, when I nudge you to dream your dream, it's not so that you can collect things; it's so you can find your way back to a feeling, an energetic vibration of inherent abundance that does not have to be earned. It just is. And when you start to feel into the vibration of abundance through meditation, affirmations, and visualization, you'll be amazed at how your life will shift. Without extra effort or forcing outcomes, you will receive gorgeous opportunities, make even more beautiful connections, and enjoy the most delicious, fulfilling, and healing experiences.

Really.

Not buying it yet?

Then let's talk about why not. We can't talk about dreams of abundance without acknowledging the part of you that might be scared to speak them aloud or that may be doubtful and skeptical that the life you envision is even possible.

If you're not allowing the dream, what is the limiting belief standing in your way?

Take out your pen again and let's reexamine what might be keeping you from allowing yourself to receive. In your own life, what are the specific obstacles in your way? What are the numbers, the data points, the logistics, the outside influences that are preventing you from living a life that feels more abundant? Write them down. Commit them to pen and paper.

What are the specific obstacles in my way for living a more abundant life?

_____

_____

_____

_____

_____

_____

_____

Once you've clarified the obstacles in your way, I want you to consider the belief that supports your obstacles. What is the story you're telling yourself about limitation? If you're not sure, consider the following:

I'll always struggle.

Eventually, I'll lose it all.

I've wasted so much time.

My dreams are too big.

I don't deserve it.

Is this true?

No. Whoever you are, these stories are not true. So the question is: Why do you believe them? What is the payoff for believing in your own limitation and not having the life you want? If your answer is, "Trust me, Cathy, there is *no* payoff. I really want my dreams to come to life," then my response would be to tell you that anytime we don't have what we truly desire, there's some resistance there. Whether you're aware of it or not, there is a payoff, there is something we each gain by staying right where we are, choosing the same life, the same circumstances, the same amount of income, the same level of success, the same type of relationships, over and over again. There is something we get out of reliving Groundhog Day. Do you know what it is? One word:

Control.

The benefit to staying right where you are is a false sense of security and control. Notice I said a "false" sense. *I know what my current reality looks like; I know what I'm dealing with so by not changing, I am safe, in control.* We say this. We think this and we often believe we're in control and that we're mitigating disappointment by repeating the same patterns and expecting less. But we're wrong. Control creates limitation because it doesn't allow for more.

When you are attached to an outcome, when you are white knuckling your way forward, when you are worried so much about how something will go, when you feel you *need* something, that's only a reflection that you are coming from a place that isn't whole. When you're in a place that needs some other thing or is dependent on some other thing to feel whole, there's a feeling of pressure and scarcity.

I'll never forget an exchange with a woman who attended one of my retreats. She said about feeling less pain and more joy, "I'd love to feel good 60 percent of the time."

I said, "Why settle for that? Imagine asking your doctor to help you relieve your nausea for only 60 percent of the day while allowing yourself to feel sick to your stomach for the remaining 40 percent. You'd never do that. Because we don't accept that."

Feeling physically good is something we all seek to feel 100 percent of the time, and if you were to tell me that you had a chronic headache or recurring nausea, I'd say, "Get yourself to the doctor! You need to get that checked out. You need to get that fixed!" In our culture, feeling physically bad is not acceptable and treatment is encouraged. But when it comes to our emotional health, we accept far less. When our lives feel hard and our energy feels depleted, too many of us shrug with acceptance: "That's just life." I reject that and so should you. Why should our expectations be any less when it comes to gauging our mental and spiritual health?

Limiting beliefs keep us stuck, keep us small, keep us sick. And it's time to set those stories down and tell a new story about our inherent worth.

BE AUDACIOUS

I want you to be audacious. I want you to have the audacity to allow yourself to let in all the things that you really want. Have the audacity. Stop making yourself wrong for wanting to allow yourself to receive more.

We all had someone in our family who said, "The other shoe's going to drop. Go easy. Don't stand out too much or don't have so much. You can lose it all." That limiting thought gets engrained in our conditioning. And very often when I'm working with someone, I'll say, "What do you want?" It's unbelievable. People can't even say what they want. What is that about?

It's amazing how we spend all this time thinking that we're working toward building this life that we came here to co-create because we're creators. And then when we stop, we think, *Yeah, I don't really give myself full permission to know that I know what I want. I know what's already here. I know that I can just allow that in.*

It's such a turn-on when you start to be that brazen, to have the audacity to talk about your standard in plain terms. What's your standard of care? What's your standard for life, for people, for humanity, for what kind of food you eat, for how you treat yourself, for how you treat other people, for boundaries? You start to have that kind of audacity and people look at you and go, *Yes. That is who I want to be.* Meanwhile, there will be people who are triggered by your audacity. So what? Those people are in their own resistance. They're going to get to the age of ninety and their time will be up in this iteration. Too bad for them. They decided that they deserve only one crumb of the cake and they judged those who ate more. That's one way to play it. You don't have to play it that way.

The more you continue to do this for yourself, the more you become a model for possibility for other people. You're a walking billboard of possibility for other people. And people go, *Yeah, there is more.* Because there are infinite realities being experienced right now. And you're choosing the one you're in.

4.

EXTERNAL NOISE

ALL MY LIFE, I loved to sing, write songs, and listen to music. Depending on what we're experiencing in our lives, music can become that accompanying soundtrack to our grief, our joy, our frustration and fears, our longings and love. All my life, I'd witnessed how music can transport people to different places and unify people who previously felt separate and alone. I moved to Los Angeles after my time in Israel with a vision that I would use my voice in a huge way. I saw myself touring the world and being a successful songwriter like Sarah McLachlan or Natalie Merchant. And while I had the vision, I struggled with the "how"—how was I going to make my dream a reality? It was bumpy at first but eventually I got the hang of it.

At the start, I had limited contacts and experience, but my desire to write and sing my songs fueled my entrepreneurial spirit and my drive to *go for it*, and with patience and steady persistence, I secured a gig at Genghis Cohen on Fairfax Avenue, a kitschy NYC-style Chinese restaurant with a small theater in the back. When I wasn't scheduled there, I sang at the Hotel Café, another small and popular space that showcased up-and-coming singer-songwriters, and when I wasn't on either stage, some friends and I started recording songs in our home studios. For clarity, a "home studio" typically meant a laptop with GarageBand. Not before too long, I was performing up to five nights a week and meeting people who knew people in the music industry. My big break came when one of my demo recordings found its way into the hands of Ron Fair, a bigwig at Interscope Records. It was a track that I'd composed for an upcoming Jim Henson TV show. When I explained the concept to Ron, he said, "Well, then, let's make a full record that can accompany the show." I was over the moon—I'd landed a record deal—and we began recording right away. I vividly remember the day I sat with Lady Gaga (Lady Gaga!) at Sunset Sounds, where she was recording a special version of "Paparazzi" for the Video Music Awards, and I thought, *Oh my God, I've made it. An intern just took my Starbucks order. This is my moment. I have arrived.*

And then, about six weeks after my big break, I was driving my little blue Saab on the busy I-10 freeway through LA when Ron called.

He said, "Hey, are you driving?"

"Yeah, I'm just passing Bundy and Olympic."

"Okay, call me when you get home or once you're off the freeway."

"I can talk now."

He paused. "It's kind of important."

I suddenly had that sinking feeling, the one that tells you to pull off the freeway and park on the side of the road. "What is it?" I asked with trepidation.

"You know we all love you," Ron said. "You've got so much good energy. We love your music. But we're just not sure that any of these songs are going to be radio singles. So . . ." He hesitated. "We're gonna drop you from the label. And we wish you all the best."

Hold up? Did he just say that he was dropping me from the label? He did not just say that, did he? When the words finally sank in, I felt like I'd been drop-kicked. I hung up and sobbed in my car until my sunblock ran into my eyes to the point I couldn't see. *What now? Where do I go from here?* I couldn't see the road in front of me, literally.

The next day, I dusted myself off. I still had the Jim Henson project, so I refocused on that until I mustered the courage to pitch myself to another label, Atlantic Records. Miraculously, they signed me . . . only to drop me a few weeks later to the same tune as Interscope: we're looking for radio standouts, like a Kelly Clarkson or another Lady Gaga. You're great, they assured me, but we need a sure hit single. At every turn, I felt like my dream to be a recording artist was so close yet continued to be just out of reach. Whatever I did, I couldn't quite catch up with my vision to share my music with the world.

At this point, many of my friends sat me down and broke the news: "Cathy, it's so sweet that you want to pursue your dream, but those things don't just happen. It's time to grow up and get a real job. Be practical. Be realistic." A well-intentioned friend of mine suggested that I pivot away from "rewarding" work and focus on making a lot of money instead. "Get into commercial real estate," she advised. "There's so much money there." I considered it and thought, *Why not?* Making money sounded good, so I put my feelers out to friends and family who might know someone who knew someone. Less than a week later, my sister called me with promising news. She'd met a man working her waitress shift at the Cheesecake Factory. They'd gotten to talking as he waited for his table, and when he shared that he owned a chain of high-end shopping centers, she offered—"My sister is hoping to get into commercial real estate!"

"Well, have her give me a call," he said. "I'm looking for someone with a great personality to help set up meetings for me."

I didn't have any experience in the field of real estate, but that didn't matter to this business owner. After he interviewed me for an hour, he said, "I love your energy. The rest you'll learn." I took him on his word and a year and a half later, at age twenty-five, I was able to trade in my little Saab for a two-door Mercedes CLK. I splurged on a couch from Anthropologie, I ordered spicy tuna rolls for lunch three times a week, and my colleagues and my boss all congratulated me. In their words, I was "crushing it."

Meanwhile, I was miserable. One morning, I saw myself in the mirrored doors of the office elevator. I was in high heels, wearing a pencil skirt and a double-breasted jacket with my hair blown out, and I started to cry because I didn't recognize the person in the mirror. I didn't recognize *me*. And furthermore, what happened to *my dream*? I knew I didn't come to LA to help rich men buy investment properties. I didn't spend three years in Israel searching for meaning just to sell my soul. How did I get so far from myself? In a flash, I thought about my own mother who'd given up her dream of performing on Broadway, a dream that she'd left behind in order to be "practical," "realistic," and a "good" wife and mother. Throughout my life, I was painfully aware that my mother's dreams had gathered dust and were dying inside of her heart. I could feel how unfulfilled she'd become, and I witnessed how deeply she struggled. I wasn't about to make a similar choice. I learned from my mother that no spouse can hand you a feeling of fulfillment. No child or white picket fence can give it to you either, because fulfillment comes from within, from servicing from a place of authenticity, from expressing yourself fully. I went into my boss's office and said, "I have to quit my job to save my life because I don't know who I am anymore." That was the day *everything changed*.

I drove away from the office, and I remembered Rabbi Aaron saying that no one wants to be out of service. We each have a gift and we want to use it. He'd said, "Imagine a guitar that's holding a potted plant in it as opposed to being used for music. It's not supposed to hold a plant; it's meant to be played." I felt like that. I knew I had so much more to give, and I felt so frustrated that the path hadn't yet unfolded for me to do what I knew I was meant to do. I decided to return to what I had learned about the radio. If all possibilities always exist, I could find a way to get paid to do music, the same way I manifested the real estate job. After all, the opportunities are already there hidden in plain sight, waiting to be revealed.

CATCHING THE DREAM

After I lost my two record deals and realized that I'd been looking outside myself to make my dream happen and believing that fulfillment was on *the other side* of my dream—I shifted my thoughts. I changed my tune. I remembered something motivational speaker Tony Robbins had said: "Our greatest resource is our resourcefulness." I repeated this quote in my mind until I became so excited, so motivated by the power within me to realize my dream with no external strings attached. Once I turned down the song of helplessness and turned *up* the lyric of empowerment, I formed new questions: If I'm not going to get a record deal, how else can I get my music into the world? What if there is another way, another channel, that I haven't seen yet? Show me another possibility. Within a week of shifting my internal inquiry—What if there's another path? What if *my* music is meant to be experienced in a different way?—I came across an article in *Billboard* magazine about indie artists who were licensing their music to TV and film, writing songs for shows like *Grey's Anatomy* and commercials for brands like Old Navy and Tropicana. As I read the article, my jaw dropped. I had never considered pitching my songs to television shows or commercials. I didn't even know creating music in that way was a possibility, and now that I did, I was determined to follow it wherever it would take me.

I began taking big risks to realize my new dream. I still got nervous, still got nudged by cortisol-pumping thoughts like *Who am I to write songs for a hit TV show?* In situations when I struggled—and when I still do—I remembered love. I thought, *No matter who the person is or how "important" they are, everyone wants love and connection. Everyone wants empathy and presence from another person.* We can always lean into that, and when we do, the fear lifts, because it's not about needing approval but about giving kindness. I thought, *Instead of making it about me, I'll pivot toward them: How can I be of service? How can I contribute? How can I make a connection? How can I support someone today and grow at the same time?* After learning about the opportunity to license my music, I googled the names of television executives at NBC, ABC, and Netflix, as well as people working for ad agencies like Leo Burnett, Deutsch, and Ogilvy and started cold-calling them. I introduced myself, told them about the music I liked to write, and asked if they were interested in licensing my songs for TV and film. I also sent an email blast to a list of music supervisors, people who specifically chose music for television shows and ads. Again, I introduced myself and offered them Mochas and Music with the following invitation:

1. Email me your Starbucks order.
2. On an appointed date and time, I'll show up with your fave coffee drink and play you a song from my new record.
3. You continue your workday happy and caffeinated.

Some ignored the offer, some said they were too busy, and a handful of people took me up on it. I'll never forget after one of my first "serenades" when the female exec behind the desk said, "So, generally, what kind of songs do you like to write?"

I responded, "What kind of songs do you need?"

She looked at me with confusion. "No one ever asks me that." Her face lit up like she was being seen for the first time all day. "Thank you," she said.

I said, "How about I write the perfect song for the story you are telling. Do you need a story about sisters, about friendship, about a reunion or a birthday?"

"Oh my God, yes, I need all of those songs."

"Great. I can write whatever you need."

And I did. I continued to put my desire for connection in front of my confidence and over time, more and more people asked to meet with me, and as soon as I started speaking the language of abundance—of possibility and creativity, of the transformative power of high vibrational music—they ate it up. My ability to align their needs with what I created expanded my client base in exciting ways. I realized that business is relationships and what makes relationships successful is radical empathy. Music is collaborative by nature. Even if you write and perform your own songs, the voice and lyrics and instruments must intertwine and align. That's how you create the most beautiful melodies. I learned quickly that when I harmonized with my clients' needs—in other words, when I empathized with their situations and created solutions to their problems through my music—not only did they want to hire me but also they offered to pay me generously, more than I would have ever dreamed of being paid. The first song I licensed sold for $58,000! Not $58—*$58,000*. And on and on it went from there. I made half a million dollars in a single year, writing songs I was able to sing myself, licensing music for shows like *One Tree Hill*, *Switched at Birth*, *Younger*, and *Pretty Little Liars* and songs for brands like Walmart and McDonald's—all on my own, DIY-style, without an agent. In just a few years after I'd lost my record deals to Interscope and Atlantic, I was featured in *Billboard* magazine, *L.A. Weekly*, and *Variety* as the "tunesmith novice [who became the] licensing guru" and "Indie artist, writing her own check." This time I had arrived because I was doing work that I would have done for free because I loved it that much.

I learned so much from the experience. Once I was making a living from my music, I realized I had been carrying this belief earlier in my life that it was either Beyoncé or bust. As if I were watching the movie of my own life, I recognized that in pursuing my dream initially, in scene after scene after scene I was waiting for someone to walk on screen and choose me, to applaud my creative efforts and award me with a platform for my music—a bright and shiny record deal—and that once this special someone granted my special wish, my life would be everything I wanted it to be. Finally, my life would match my dream.

In that moment of clarity, I nearly laughed out loud.

What was I doing? Waiting on someone else to make my dreams for me? Waiting on something outside of myself to fulfill me? This limiting belief hit me like a double whammy. How had I not seen it before? I unconsciously believed that fulfillment was on the other side of achieving my dream *and* I was looking for someone else's validation to make that dream happen. Did you get that? It took me a minute too.

I believed that my fulfillment was determined by a certain level of achievement, and I thought someone else had to give me permission to do the things I loved.

What happened next was unexpected.

Other aspiring songwriters, creatives in the music and entertainment fields, and most anyone with a dream would read about me in a magazine and send me emails asking, "What's your secret?"

People started asking me to teach them how to make money from their creative pursuits, which was a surprise. I started a workshop in my living room for ten people. The class had so much demand that I wound up renting a theater for one hundred people and soon we needed a theater big enough for four hundred. After a year of successfully teaching sold-out classes, someone suggested I start an online course.

At first, I was hesitant. I knew nothing about the digital space whatsoever. In fact, I had an aversion to online marketing and online business because I thought it was just a bunch of bros selling snake oil.

But it dawned on me that I could reach more people if I taught them online, so I found a woman named Amy Porterfield who taught a course about creating online courses. Fast-forward a couple of months and I decided to launch my first online course for songwriters. I had no idea what I was doing, but I just trusted that if I took one imperfect step at a time, I would be led to whatever was meant to be.

I was pregnant with my third daughter, and I launched the messy version of my first course in July, since my baby was due in September. I wasn't worried about it being perfect. I had never done a webinar before—I didn't make a single slide—but I showed up with heart and spoke directly to every single face on the screen. I made $147,000 that night alone. It was an amazing feeling, and I knew it was just the beginning.

I did a second launch of the course again three months later and made $440,000. Within twelve months, I made my first million, and—can you believe it?—one of my first course students was the one to suggest I start a podcast. I started the podcast in my closet with my three-week-old baby sitting beside me. I didn't have a social media presence at the time or an email list. The podcast grew to almost fifty million downloads and helped me reach people all over the world. I started to teach more of the spiritual side of things and help people begin a meditation practice. We were featured by Apple Podcasts multiple times and nominated for a Webby award. I got my first book deal and began coaching thousands of women a year. This led to a zillion more amazing opportunities.

People always ask me how to get there, and my answer then and now remains the same—sure, there's a strategy to employ, practical pieces to put into place, and a solid work ethic to embrace when you're building any business—but, at the end of the day, whatever your dream or aspiration, it really comes down to offering to the world your *energy*, your vibration. Where are you tuned on the radio dial? Truly, I cannot emphasize this enough: if you're wondering why you're not having more breakthroughs, why the money isn't coming in, why the love isn't pouring in behind you, look at your energy. If you're feeling defeated, it's because you're somehow in resistance to the blessings that are all around you. Perhaps you don't believe it's possible or you are disappointed that it hasn't happened yet. When you're not in resonance with a higher energetic state, you hold yourself apart from receiving more.

If you're not in resonance, you cannot receive.

Dr. Lisa Miller is a professor at Columbia and a clinical psychologist, best known for her research into spirituality in psychology. She shared a beautiful visualization with me when she came on the podcast. She said to think of your life journey as a path to a big red door.

You go right up to your red door, you grab the handle, but it's stuck. And you perhaps can't believe it's stuck because you had done everything right. You kick the door. It doesn't move. You're angry, maybe depressed. But only because it is stuck. You have no choice. You pivot, you pivot, and you turn 20, 50 degrees, a hairpin turn. And there is a radiant, wide open yellow door. You might have said yellow doors don't exist. You've not heard of yellow doors. You cross the threshold and there is something more right for you. There is a community where you feel alive and connected. There is a job or an internship that opens up a side of yourself you didn't know you even had. That yellow door led to a land that was not what you had wanted. It was better than what you had wanted, and better for you. And as you step back and think about that stuck red door, the hairpin turn leading to the yellow door—there's so much to do with who you are and where you are today. Was there anyone there at the hairpin to turn it? Maybe somebody you met for two minutes on the bus or at a party? Maybe there was somebody you've known for years, a dear friend, a grandparent who shared a story they've

never shared before. Someone pointed the way and gave you information to the yellow door. They were an angel along the path to
bring you to the hairpin turn.

There are so many yellow doors on our path that might've seemed insignificant. If you actually look back at your life, there have been a series of
those yellow doors. Those are the things that we have no control over. And
that is called synchronicity. That is the great big oneness of the field. That is
the universe, this web that we're all connected to that we think we're separate from. How cool to know this is all happening.

For me, my yellow door was my interest in meditation and my spiritual
practice, which I thought I was just doing for my own sanity. I had no idea I
would eventually be called to share it. I started teaching meditation around
2009, when I took a break from songwriting. I thought, *Sure, I'll teach meditation.* And then I went back into songwriting full time, but the universe had
other plans.

We think we have to know and we have to control every aspect of our
lives, but you don't know who you'll end up meeting tomorrow, what conversation you'll have that could lead to a book deal or a podcast or a seed of
an idea. The truth is, there is a great known. You're in it. You're being guided
by it. It's all around us all the time. Let go of trying to control how it needs to
be or what you think you need to know; just flow.

WHEN I STOPPED outsourcing my dream and refocused my thoughts on
abundance and a belief in myself, the process of receiving became *so much
fun.* Every day, I was writing music, I was doing what I loved to do most, I
was radiating the lightness of my own being; as a result, I began receiving
from the external world at the rate of my internal frequency, at the rate of
my vitality and my own life source. And that's how I finally caught up with

my dream. I stopped chasing it and started enjoying the music that was within me all along. Not externally and in the future. Internally and now.

I believed that dream fulfillment happened externally and in the future. Not internally and now.

Does this resonate with you too? When you really look at your own patterns, do you find that you often wait for something outside yourself to make you feel good and whole on the inside? So many of us believe that if we had more money in the bank, we'd feel successful. We believe that if that person finally called and asked us out, we'd feel loved. We believe that if we reached our goal or achieved the thing we've always wanted to achieve, we would finally be able to sit back and exhale with ease . . . *Look at that, I finally did it. I have arrived.* The falsity of this thinking is that the future does not guarantee anything. Imagine your disappointment to finally "arrive" and realize that your dream wasn't waiting for you, and that in all the years leading up to this future moment, you'd forgotten to live in the present.

IF/WHEN . . .

Take a moment and pull out a pen and paper. Write down your favorite "If I get it" or "When this happens . . . I'll be happy" stories. For example, *I'll be happy when I'm making more money.* Or, *If only I could find love, I would feel fulfilled.*

I'll be happy when _____.

If and when _____ happens, I will feel fulfilled.

As you form your answers, become aware of your tendency to externalize your happiness, to put your sense of fulfillment and well-being in the hands of others. This tendency is often unconscious, so be gentle with yourself. The other habit that many of us have (again, without realizing it) is to blame outside circumstances—the stock market, the weather, the new hire in the corner office—for affecting and dictating our day and for ultimately standing in our way. These tendencies deny us our own agency, our own power. They tune us to the channel of helplessness.

Return to your pen and paper. Write down your frequently told "If so-and-so would get out of my way . . . I'd be happy" stories. For example, *I could go after my dream if my partner made more money.* Or, *If the cost of living wasn't so high, I would be happier.*

If _____ would/wouldn't
_____, I could finally pursue my dream.

If _____ changed, then I would feel different.

Look at your answers. Do you notice the ways in which you're outsourcing your sense of feeling good, outsourcing your fulfillment, your sense of abundance? So many of us fall into this trap. We tell ourselves that happiness happens only *after* something external, something we don't already have, shows up at our door. Or we tell ourselves that happiness happens only after something external that we already have and no longer want exits stage right. This focus on a future outcome creates a feeling of lack in the present.

It creates a feeling of discontent in your life, right now. And not only that, when the obstacle is removed and you do get the job promotion, meet someone new, go on the dream vacation, or buy the house—what happens then? You feel good, you feel *great* . . . then five days, five weeks, or five months later, the sense of excitement and novelty wears off and you start searching for that *feeling* again. Maybe you'll find it somewhere else, you think, and so you go searching for the feeling, believing that it is somewhere in the future, somewhere outside of you, somewhere other than where you are, and you continue to seek it out. I know from experience that this search is exhausting and can become ultimately frustrating when it feels like, no matter what you do, you're always on the other side of your dreams. But here's the thing—that's not how it works. That feeling you seek is not dependent on external circumstances because it's within you, and it's available in this moment. That's right, and I'm going to say it again: the feeling you seek is not dependent on external circumstances because it's within you, and it's available in this moment.

That piece that's in your blind spot—*that* is the part that must be healed. And you're the only person who can provide that healing.

And believe me, there can be a lot of fun and joy in that healing.

The satisfaction that you take with you every day that you live is in bumping up against new problems to solve and finding new courage in yourself, or finding more resourcefulness in yourself, or being able to come up with a way to allow more ease where you weren't a second ago. That is literally where the joy comes from.

If you were climbing a mountain, were halfway up, and somebody said, "Oh, I'll just take you up in a helicopter," you would hate it, because a big part of the satisfaction comes from climbing the mountain yourself and achieving what you thought was possible. That overrides the part of you that wants to give up, to quit before the summit. That's the whole joy of the journey, because you're not chasing the outcome. You're chasing the feeling of integrity and the courage to reach and surpass your potential. Think of it this way: when you show up in yoga class with tight hamstrings and you push yourself to hold the pose for seven seconds longer than you did before—that's the feeling you're chasing.

Every day there are plenty of opportunities to grab that feeling. That feeling is always available to you. And this is what's cool about any journey, right? It's never about the goal. It's always about who we become by working toward it.

So often we look outside ourselves for the expansion that lives within.

The feelings we all seek—ease, well-being, love, peace, connection, meaning, and joy—are available to every one of us *right now* because our true Self is always feeling well-being. Our true Self is the part of us beyond our personality, beyond our habitual thoughts, beliefs, and behaviors. Our true Self is the essence of who we are. The true Self is who we were at conception, that essential authentic soul within that is that aspect of us that is always our authentic spirit. We are always connected, a breath away. And when we learn to recognize that connection, we become able to put our hand on the receiver that allows us to tune into the frequency we seek.

So how do we tap into that? What is the practice?

The practice is every single day when you get up, you practice coming home to the truth that you are more than the persona you pretend to be. You are so much more than your body, where you went to college, what you weigh, or the zip code you live in. Remind yourself, "I am a soul."

There's this place inside of you that feels like your highest self, your truth, your center, your soul. Every morning, align with that part of you that isn't trying to compete, that feels totally enough.

Here's how you do it. Feel in. Close your eyes. Put your hand on your heart. Take a deep breath . . . and find your center.

Take a couple deep breaths.

Find the you of you.

The you of you is the part of you that feels connected to endless love, endless compassion, strength, wisdom, grace, kindness, expansion.

Can you feel that? That part of you—that's where you lead from. And we need to practice being anchored in that.

Psychologist Dr. Rick Hanson shared with me a Buddhist proverb about ghosts with empty bellies who are insatiable; they're always craving something, and they're never satisfied. Day after day, they go on eating and eating and eating and just as they're about to feel full, they say, "I'm still hungry; give me the next thing."

That feeling of insatiability is one we've all experienced, don't you agree?

We begin to think that the bigger the pile of stuff we have, the richer we'll feel. We begin to think that if we can just get the right stuff, we will feel safe and in control. But the deepest satisfaction we feel is always and only determined by how we feel within ourselves.

When we can tune into this higher love, connection, and alignment, we have everything we've been seeking. The wealthiest people have an inner world that is rich, and the reality they live in will always reflect that.

The Dalai Lama is a great example of internalized well-being, of controlling the one thing he can: his thoughts, his inner life. His serenity, his warmth, the wonder and joy communicated through his eyes is not because

His Holiness just scored a bag of cash. He is not being lit from the outside; his light radiates from within. To look at photographs or video of him, you can quite literally see light pouring outward from him, and while the Dalai Lama is an exceptional human being and one of the highest spiritual leaders of our time, we all have the capacity to find lightness in our own being. To find joy in *what is*.

I'm serious.

You may think that a life of abundance will only happen when you get the corner office or the convertible that allows the wind to blow through your hair. You may think that, but that feeling is available right now, wherever you are, whether you're driving a luxury car or run-down Toyota and whatever the state of your hair, because there's no moment in the future that's better than this moment. Better *later* doesn't exist because what you're waiting for is the feeling you think you'll feel in the future and that can exist right now. Why would you wait for something to happen in order to give yourself the permission to feel that good when you can feel every good feeling right now? Truly, whoever you are, you can feel better now. You can find the feeling of joy, love, freedom all within your being. And when you feel better, you do better. The Dalai Lama doesn't just radiate light, he performs tremendous acts of service, and we're each capable of the same. We each have the capacity to connect with and transform the lives of so many people, and it starts with ourselves. It starts by changing the dial. By developing an awareness of our thoughts and beliefs and how they affect the *frequency* of our lives.

How we choose to perceive reality is the only thing we really have any control over.

THE SOUNDTRACK WITHIN

Picture this: you walk into a store or your favorite restaurant and you immediately tune into the music playing overhead. Whether you're shopping for a new pair of jeans or ordering your two-taco lunch, the frequency and *feeling* of the music can make or break your experience, right? As an example of "making it," I recently started dancing in the changing room of one of my favorite boutiques when the woman behind the register turned up the volume on a remix of Whitney Houston singing "Higher Love." As I was trying on pants and tops and belts, I started singing along and feeling so dang good in my body that I could hardly stand it. It's no secret that I love me some great music—Pentatonix, Ben Rector, Rachel Platten, Sara Bareilles are just a few of my many favorites. Music is a transportation device. In less than three minutes, a song can take you to a different place. Truly, music can blast you through the confines of three-dimensional time and space and lift you to a higher place. When I hear those soulful, energetic lyrics, I cannot help myself—I go higher; I automatically align with the elevated frequency of the music. Our energy becomes a match, and it's magnetic!

TUNE IN AND TURN UP!

We best hear the music on the channel we are tuned into, so in this next exercise, you will tune into yourself, into your energetic vibration. This sounds simple enough because, think about it: most of us know, without even looking, how much battery we have left on our iPhone or smartphone, but the same doesn't hold true for our internal battery. Are you operating at 10 percent or 90 percent? Are you dipping into the red or are you fully charged? Do you know?

Most of us pay more attention to our external devices than to *ourselves*, and how are you going to align with the elevated frequency of someone like Whitney Houston or Meghan Trainor if your own battery is dying? You won't! You can't!

Before you can upshift your energy, you need to know where you're starting. This requires awareness, becoming conscious of where you've been unconscious. One of the best ways I've found to do this is to set a reminder on my phone that nudges me three to four times a day to check in. At the top of the hour, up pops the reminder: time to check my vibration. How do I feel? I'll stop what I'm doing, take a deep breath, and invite the feeling to rise from within me. And once I feel it, I name it.

Try it. Set an alarm to go off three to four times a day on your favorite device, and when it goes off, ask yourself: What's my energy level? How am I feeling? What channel am I listening to?

Vague answers like "fine," "good," "not great," or "the oldies station" do not count. Identify a descriptive feeling and note the feeling by writing it down or recording it in some way (this is important!). Also, be specific about whether your feeling is rooted in a song about the past, the present, or the future, and whether it is a positive melody—happy, content, grateful, loved, purposeful, creative, and so on—or a chorus brooding with disappointment, anger, or lack. As you record your energy level and your feeling state, resist the urge to judge whatever comes up. Instead, regard your feelings as *visitors* that will knock at the door, and knock at the door, louder and louder until you let them in. Some visitors stay for an hour, for a cup of tea. Some visitors sleep overnight. And then, usually, in the morning, they will go. Maybe they'll stick around for longer, because feelings need to be seen and witnessed, but they will eventually pass on because feelings are also energy in motion. They need to move. Don't be afraid of what you feel. Roll out the welcome mat for whatever is at the door. Make space for these feelings and eventually they'll say goodbye because no feeling sticks around forever.

Right now, on a scale of 1–5, my energy is at a _____ .

When I relate my energy level to a feeling, I can name it as ____
_____ .

My feelings are rooted in the past, present, or future [choose one].

Getting into the habit of checking in with your energy and feelings is a powerful practice. To take it one step further, after you identify the feeling, and the time frame of the feeling, attempt to trace it to a specific thought.

Energy >>>>> Feeling >>>>> Thought

Right now, I'm feeling _____ ,
and that feeling is tied to this thought: _____
_____ .

Every second of the day our minds run on autopilot and play a pattern of old thoughts on repeat. Most of our thoughts are the same thoughts we had the day before. Our life doesn't change because we are thinking, feeling, and behaving the same way we've always done, which means we have the same vibrational imprint, and we manifest the same results. Things don't change unless we start to change the way we think, perceive, and behave. Essentially, until we let go of past emotional addictions, we won't create a new manifestation.

While thoughts are key, let's not forget that feelings create our thoughts. Whether you know it or not, you have feelings all the time. Most of them are unconscious and take up a lot of space in your life. We often can't perceive these unconscious feelings because we're not in touch with them. Have you ever seen someone's anger skyrocket from zero to sixty for no rational reason? You see it and think, *My gosh, how did that happen?* Well, it's because they were thinking and believing and feeling a lot of things of which they weren't aware. Maybe it was a feeling they're still holding on to from when their dad died, or from a bad breakup when they were eighteen years old, or from losing a job years before. Regardless of the cause, the truth is they're not aware. They can't even perceive that they're thinking and feeling any of it.

For us to co-create, design, and manifest what we actually want, we have to start becoming conscious of what all those feelings are—and stop unconsciously feeling the slog of these negative feelings all the time. The mind will always have a negativity bias; the more we normalize that and anticipate it, the less we get caught in it. Those bad feelings are going to spit out negative thought flurries, and we're constantly making things in our lives out of that snow, whether we know it or not. The more we open the aperture, the more we open up the awareness that will bring us into alignment. Then, based on our alignment and our truth, we can select what we know to be true, as opposed to just creating these little snow creatures. We act on the positive feelings of our higher self and create the life we want.

BEYOND THE THOUGHTS: YOUR NERVOUS SYSTEM

There have been countless books written about positive thinking and mindset. While that's great, we have so much more to understand about what is creating the ease and manifestations in our life, and it goes beyond the conversation around positive thinking.

We're really not taught this. The nervous system is either regulated, which means you feel a sense of calm and purpose, or dysregulated, which makes you feel agitated and out of control. At any moment, there's either more or less calm in your nervous system. It's your nervous system that's going to decide and dictate what the thoughts are going to be. Sure, you could put a Band-Aid on it and just read positive thoughts or say them to yourself. But what's going to do a more lasting job is to take a moment to check in and assess, *Where is my nervous system right now? What's happening? Am I activated? Am I regulated? Do I feel ease? Or do I feel something happening on a visceral level that feels a little bit out of balance?* That is really where all this work begins, because your vibration is an extension of what's happening internally.

That is why meditating or taking a walk is so important to lead us back into a place where there is more ease and equilibrium. Once we have that safety, we can go beyond the body into where all creativity exists, where the ideas and divine downloads come from.

When I was first introduced to meditation, I thought it meant sitting in silence devoid of all thought, like floating in an empty fish tank, just water and pretty plankton. I'm not kidding—when I was invited to my first meditation retreat by a friend from my old Jim Henson days, at the UCLA Mindful Awareness Research Center in 2008, I thought, *How bad could it be?* I'll tell you—very bad. Less than an hour into the eight-hour experience, I felt like I'd been locked in a torture chamber where my skin was being peeled off. One hundred people sitting on the hard floor in complete silence was not, as it turned out, *my thing*. I'm a chatty person by nature and I was used to activity, to doing, and what was I supposed to *do* for eight hours on a yoga mat? I became bored quickly. I didn't know how to distract myself, and my thoughts were not quiet. Rather, they were spinning on repeat: *Why is this so hard? Why can't I do this? Who in their right mind likes this? This is torture. Can I leave without anyone noticing?* Eventually, I got up and left, and people noticed. As I paced outside on the UCLA campus, I worried that people were judging me—and, worse, I judged myself. I didn't want to walk out on the experience feeling defeated, the girl who couldn't stop talking or thinking for five minutes. I resigned myself to try it again, and as I walked back into the room, the meditation leader broke the silence and addressed the group with these words: "See if you can be curious about the things you are thinking. Minds wander; that's what they do. So can you watch your thoughts and ask yourself, *What will my next thought be?*"

Mic drop.

Did she just acknowledge that all these quiet people were *thinking*? Did she just give us all permission to think? You mean, I don't have to turn my mind off? I just have to watch my thoughts?

This I could do. This was interesting. Suddenly, I wasn't bored. I was engaged with my own mind, but rather than thinking mindlessly, I grew an awareness of my thoughts. I became curious about what floated in and out, and at some point, I stopped thinking—well, I stopped overthinking. I sat for the next seven hours in stillness, in contemplation, in a state of calm, and in this space, my life clicked into focus. *Click.* It was mind-blowing, and I was hooked.

As I kept practicing meditation, I noticed that once I was dropped into a place where there is attunement, then I became a vessel for so much expansion, so much awareness and perception. This state of being allows us to perceive because we're not looking through fight or flight.

When the body is dysregulated, it's in a state of fight or flight, the pupils dilate, all the blood rushes to the extremities, the heart rate accelerates a little bit, and awareness constricts. The body takes the cue and says, "Something's wrong. This isn't a great time to perceive new possibilities or allow for new perception." Side note: your immune system can't handle that for long periods. This chronic flight-or-fight stage inhibits the immune system because it doesn't know how to handle that level of fear all the time.

This is why the habit of self-care matters. It's not just a cute idea. It's essential. Whether it's taking a bath or taking a walk, expanding your capacity to nourish yourself is a direct path into manifesting. Having practices in your life that settle your body and nourish you are going to be directly responsible for what comes next, which is an awareness that was always there. You just couldn't see it before, because your mind was too busy and your body was so activated that you'd lost sight of what was right there all along.

THE POWER OF CONNECTING TO THE DIVINE

I was in a car accident when I was in college. I was sitting in the back seat and the driver had turned around so she could tell us something. When she faced forward again, she thought she was going to hit the car in front of us. She overcorrected and lost control.

We started rolling. The car was totaled, but, thank God, we all lived. I ended up with some injuries in my neck and was told I needed to have neck surgery. Two doctors told me that they needed to take bone out of my hip to fix my neck. Instead, I found my way to physical therapy and acupuncture. At one point in that journey, I decided I was going to have the surgery. I went to Jackson Memorial Hospital in Miami and saw Dr. Bart Green, the head of neurosurgery and spinal surgery. I had an MRI, and he said, "Okay, we need bone to fix this." Same story, and this time my dad offered to give the bone from his hip, which I thought was this very spiritual, important thing, because he had been out of my life for many years at this point, and now he was back and offering to do an extremely generous thing for me. I booked the surgery just as I found out Rabbi Aaron was going to be in Florida hosting a retreat. I really wanted to go. My doctor advised me not to drive, and I said, "Well, I'm not going to drive. I'll be in the passenger seat." He shook his head. "I still don't recommend that you drive an hour in the car. What if you get hit by another car? Your neck is in a really bad spot."

I said, "I'm going, I'm going, I'm going." And when I went, I asked for a blessing that the surgery would go well. And what did Rabbi Aaron do? He had the two hundred people at his retreat close their eyes and send me this open-hearted, loving energy so that everything would go well. There was not even a thought of *she doesn't need it*. Let's heal her. Two days later, I went in to have the surgery, and my doctor requested that I have one more MRI. It was a closed MRI that took an hour and a half, and they moved my neck into all types of positions. When I came out of the MRI, the doctor said to the nurse, "Where are her films?" and she said, "This is the film." He did a double-take. "This is someone else's film," he said. "There's no problem with this neck." They went back and forth like this until he finally turned to me. "Cathy, you don't need surgery. What did you do? What happened since you last saw me?"

I shrugged. "I went to a healing retreat."

"Come back in six weeks," he said. "Maybe it was a fluke." I kept coming back. I was fine, and is that crazy or what?

Being in a relationship with God isn't just healing for the physical body; it also has amazing contributions to strengthening our minds. Dr. Lisa Miller told me how when she was a young intern she facilitated an inpatient unit at a psychiatric hospital. She was surrounded by psychiatrists and psychologists who were good, smart people who were well trained in their field. But she said there was not a whisper about spirituality. In fact, it was considered provocative to even make a peep about spirituality or religion. And yet, she saw that patients were hungry for it. They would ask her to pray with them in the back pantry because they felt it was so forbidden.

As Dr. Lisa tells it,

What we see is breathtaking. My team has used MRI genotyping, long term, you name it. We've pulled out every lens we have in clinical science. And it is simply the case that we are innately spiritual beings. This is who we are.

There are two forms of relational spirituality. One is transcendent—to be in connection to our higher power—and the other is imminent—to feel our higher power in one another and fellow living beings. This is how we're built, and over twenty years, we've been published in top peer-reviewed journals with evidence that is absolutely clear as a bell: when we strengthen our natural birthright, we are far less likely to be addicted, depressed, to take our lives, and far more likely to live in a deep dialogue with spirit through which life is much more inspired.

At the level of an MRI scan, we see broad regions of the brain, regions of perception, reflection, and orientation. The occipital is thick and strong. The cortex is processing power. We have a better brain. We have a more capable brain of seeing and perceiving when we cultivate over time, a spiritual response to suffering, a spiritual way of engaging times of emptiness.

THE MORE TIME YOU SPEND arriving at your own door, drinking in the wholeness of this moment, the more you become regulated and coherent. This coherence starts to move in the world, and people will feel more regulated around you because you are. They'll have better ideas when they're with you, because you become something that they can tether to. It's your vibration, your very being that becomes something that allows them to find a way into their own stream.

As we become conscious of our thoughts and feelings, we begin to clear static from our vibration so that we can become a clear channel for possibility, for new opportunities, for the life we've always dreamed. Too many of us spend our days on automatic, listening to the same songs of limitation and tuning into external noise. Once you're aware of the music you're moving to, you can consciously change your tune.

5.

TEST YOUR LIMITS

THE NEXT STEP to changing your dial is to recognize that your reality is created through your beliefs. I like to say things twice, so they really sink in: the next step to changing your dial is to recognize that your reality is created through your beliefs.

Did that sink in?

Let's dig a little deeper into beliefs. What is a belief, anyway? It's a thought you've thought so many times, a thought you've repeated to the point you don't realize you're even *thinking* it that eventually, over time, you believe without question. And because your life is a mirror image—a hologram, if you will—of your thoughts, whatever you're kicking around in that head of yours creates your life. So, if there's something in your life that's not working or that you don't want, or if there's something missing from your life that you long for, there is a belief, or two or three or four, standing in your way, interfering with your ability to *receive*, to tune into the life you most desire. We'll dig into the beliefs that create the biggest static in our lives later. For now, simply consider this—the life where you have enough money to buy a home or take a beach vacation, where you're mentally strong and physically thriving, where you're connected to your community, happy with your work, your family, yourself—this life where all potentials exist is waiting for you as soon as you tune into its *frequency.*

You can change a belief like changing the radio dial.

THE MOST POPULAR STATION ON THE DIAL

Too many of us are tuned to the channel of limitation because we've been listening to it for so long, we didn't realize we could listen to something else. Can you imagine a world where you only listened to smooth jazz, not realizing that you could be swaying to the sultry beats of salsa? I shudder at the thought. Let me tell you why we get stuck on one channel. Ninety-five percent of our brains are made up of the subconscious, which means that nearly the entirety of our brain is hardwired into a set of beliefs that were programmed at an early age, typically by our parents, other family members, and other adults in our lives, such as teachers, mentors, and caregivers, and let's not forget the influence of television and other media.

We don't often realize it, but most of us are "running software" that was programmed into our subconscious minds before we turned six or seven years old. At the time, this program was likely doing an important job—protecting you and keeping you safe from whatever sticky situations were making you feel that you needed to "run this program" to survive.

In some cases, people adopt beliefs to keep them safe from real physical harm, and in other cases, we adopt beliefs to help us understand our lives and find a place to "fit" within them. In my early childhood home, I adopted a belief that my worth was validated by saving my mom and becoming perfect for my dad. Believing this and operating from this belief was how I fit into my family dynamic and survived a toxic household. My dear friend Ben grew up with a different set of circumstances that informed his early beliefs. He was a child in a modest household where his mom stayed at home and his father worked hard as an independent bookseller. When Ben was thirteen, his dad died unexpectedly, leaving Ben and his mom and sister not only in deep grief but also struggling financially. For the next five years, Ben slept on the floor of his mother's cramped, rent-controlled apartment; after he graduated from public high school, he put himself through college and then law school and business school by working and taking out student loans and saving as much as possible. He became a lawyer and then a vice president of his company; still, his early experiences formed a limiting belief in him that he couldn't shake, a belief that the world is unpredictable and resources are limited, and that in order to play it safe—to live a life that is stable and secure—a person must always hold their money close.

It makes sense, doesn't it, that he would navigate his life this way? And it similarly makes sense why I would unconsciously believe that a "good mother" always puts her family first, because the brain of a young child is like a sponge, soaking up what it hears about the world, including beliefs on the wide spectrum of abundance and limitation. And sponges, like young minds, don't filter. They soak it all up without question or critical thought. The young mind doesn't ask, "Is this true? Could there be another way to see this?" If the young mind hears "In this family, we work hard for our money" or "People with big houses are greedy" or "There's never enough" or "Things don't work out for us," it translates these statements as facts, and like a well-worn pair of Birkenstocks that conform to your feet, these so-called facts create well-worn neural pathways in our minds that become the basis for our limiting beliefs. There's good reason why you hardwire your own set of beliefs into your unconscious, and now I'm nudging you to wake up, to become conscious of what you believe and how you operate so that instead of running an old program that no longer works for you, and is likely out of date and unnecessary, you can upgrade your software (that is, your beliefs) to reflect a more expansive life.

TUNE INTO YOUR BELIEFS

Like our awareness of our energy, most of us are also unaware of what our beliefs are on a deep level, and it's these subconscious beliefs that run the show—influencing how we feel. Again, it's all connected.

Get still and take a real hard look into how you feel about abundance. How available are you for flow if it points you toward something unexpected? How safe does it feel to release control and free yourself to be totally abundant? You will get an answer immediately. Your life is a reflection of what does feel available, and you'll notice right away. For some people, the answer is, "Wow, it really doesn't feel safe to have an unclear plan." If that's how you feel right now, that's okay. You don't even have to know why. This is about recognizing your relationship with that energy. You need to understand where you are in order to open your eyes to what *is*.

From this place, it is time to plug in. It is time to start adjusting the radio dial to find your frequency. It is as simple as coming into that energy and seeing if you can move this energy just 1 percent or 5 percent. From that place, you start to come back into alignment. And in your alignment, you have full safety. You are safe to receive. You're safe to be abundant. You are safe to be in flow, period.

If you look through the eyes of your soul, you'll realize, *Wow, I haven't even scratched the surface of how much capacity I have to just let go, to enjoy it, to receive, to just be humble and say thank you.* You really are here to just keep deepening and broadening the greater vessel within you. That's your only work.

WHEN MY HUSBAND and I were first dating, he would do something supportive or kind. And he said, "I feel like no matter how much love I give you it's almost like there's a bucket with a hole in the bottom so you don't retain it. It just goes out." At that time, I didn't have the full capacity I have now to receive his love. I had to build a vessel to have it and be at peace with having it.

We often don't know how to have. We only know how to earn. We don't become a steward of contribution because we can't contribute something we don't have to contribute. We first must have it, so we must embody the safe, peaceful feeling of *having*. Often, when we say we want to enjoy and live a life of luxury and abundance, we don't have it because we don't have a vessel to hold it.

If your vessel to receive is thimble sized, you can have only as much as you can hold. If you say to yourself five times, "I am at peace with having lots of money," do you hear a response? Does your mind go *Whoa* or *I don't think so*? Or does your mind say *Yes, I am at peace with having lots of money*?

What is the feeling of being at peace with having a lot? It means experiencing the abundance that's already here and knowing that you can expand your capacity to feel all of it, because it's already here. If you're feeling lack, it's because you're not feeling the abundance that's already here because your vessel can't hold it. You could hold more if you were available to hold more.

Take a deep breath. Settle into this moment. When you feel ready, complete the following sentences, either in a journal, in the notes section of your phone, or in this book. Challenge yourself to write what immediately comes to mind without judgment or second-guessing. Read the question and then be radically honest.

Define *wealth, richness, abundance.* Are they one and the same? If not, how are they different?

_____

_____

_____

_____

_____

_____

_____

Having more abundance in my life would mean [what about me]?

_____

_____

_____

_____

What does it mean when other people live "abundant" lives?

_____

_____

_____

_____

_____

_____

_____

Do I deserve more abundance in my life? Why or why not?

_____

_____

_____

_____

_____

_____

Do I believe receiving an abundant life is my birthright? Or, conversely, do I believe that I don't deserve more than I already have?

_____

_____

_____

_____

_____

Do I believe that abundance is reserved for other people?

_____

_____

_____

_____

Take a moment to reflect on your responses. What do you notice? What came up for you?

_____

_____

_____

_____

_____

_____

_____

As you think about the meaning behind your responses, I want to share a story about my friend Rebecca. When she was twelve, her dad left her mom for a younger woman after he "struck it rich" with a business deal. From Rebecca's perspective, her father's financial windfall led him to ditch her and the life they had together to start a new family without her.

And then, without being aware of it, Rebecca grew from a young girl into an adult woman who sabotaged every career advancement and romantic relationship that came her way. One day, after breaking it off with a wealthy suitor, she offhandedly said to me, "It's all for the best, because you know that when men have a lot of money, they eventually go off the rails and break up their marriage."

I said, "Now, hold on. Let's look at that for a second. Is that true? It sounds like a story you're telling yourself, but is it true?"

"Of course, it's true," she said. "Look around. I see it happening all the time. Money corrupts relationships. It's a classic narrative."

I challenged her. "You see it happening because your mind goes looking for evidence to prove your belief to be true. But if you wanted to, you could find evidence that proves your belief false. On my podcast, for example, I've interviewed a lot of celebrities and financially secure men who have never left their marriages, and I've met a lot of women who haven't lost everything because they've chosen a partner with wealth.

"Over the years," I said, "I think you've confused a false belief with the truth, and you're not going to be able to receive abundance in love until you replace that old belief that money corrupts relationships with something else."

"Like what?" she asked, sincerely curious.

"Well, let me ask you this. When your dad left your mom, was there a part of you that felt like he was leaving you too?"

Rebecca teared up. "I guess so, yes, I felt abandoned by him too."

"What would happen if you allowed yourself to believe that you're worth loving? That you're worth sticking around for? That money has nothing to do with how much or how little you receive?"

"I'd like to believe that," Rebecca said.

I recognized Rebecca's hesitation for what it really was—at the root of her dissatisfaction was shame. So many of us feel unworthy on a level that's so insidious it keeps us from the wholeness within that's already there. We feel a deficiency, a lack, and it's usually because of what's passed down through our parents, even though—in many cases—they did the best job they could. Shame is the great illusion because it's not something inherent; it is an external force that we digest and use to create interpretations about ourselves, and it keeps us from thriving.

I said to Rebecca, "You can change your beliefs at any time. You're worthy of love. And not only from men but from yourself. Try that new belief on and see what happens."

I DON'T BELIEVE THAT, DO I?

Unconscious beliefs have a way of sneaking up on us, and I'm not immune. I've been surprised by my beliefs many times. For example, after a long struggle with infertility and several miscarriages, I was thrilled when I became pregnant with my first daughter, but I was also terrified that motherhood would jeopardize my then-growing career as a songwriter.

"How can I meet with the soundtrack departments at different studios *now*?" I asked my friend Ilaina after I'd entered my second trimester.

"What's changed? Haven't you always met directly with the studios?" she asked. "From the way you tell it, you just walk in there and ask them for what they need."

"Yes, but . . ."

"Why have you decided that being pregnant would mean you have to stop doing this or that you wouldn't be taken seriously if you walked in pregnant?" she asked.

"Um . . . um." I was speechless. I had to think about it, and what came up was an image of my own mother who gave up her own dreams for our family. As she frequently told it to me in our house growing up, before my mother met my father, she was a talented young actress. In her senior year of high school, she played the lead in a show called *Once Upon a Mattress*; the girl who played her understudy was Ellen Green. After graduation, Ellen went to audition for *Little Shop of Horrors* on Broadway, and while Mom very much wanted to pack her suitcase and head straight to New York City, she'd just met my soon-to-be-father and she believed she must make a choice, and she chose marriage and the hope of happiness behind a white picket fence. Ellen followed her passion for performing. While Mom consciously chose to stay behind with my father, Ellen landed the lead role in the Broadway show. Whenever Mom told this story, I could feel her resentment and regret, and still she continued to underscore her belief for her reasons to forgo an acting career. Mom believed that a "good" wife and mother sacrifices her personal dreams for her family, and a woman who pursues her own creative life is "bad." This is what my mom believed and even though my own marriage and family dynamic looked completely different than the one I observed in my own parents, I realized that I had unconsciously absorbed my mother's belief and customized it to an exaggerated degree: children undermine personal creativity. Family life replaces career. Motherhood undermines self-identity.

As if she were reading my thoughts, Ilaina said, "You're not your mom, you're *you*."

"I know, but—"

"Don't you want it all—motherhood and your career? You can be good at both."

"Yes," I said.

"Then *believe* that you can."

This was one of those light bulb moments for me. On a conscious level, I believed (or at least, I thought I did) that plenty of parents, and women specifically, can find a way to have a family life and professional and creative pursuits and an intact sense of self. But on an unconscious level, Mom's limiting beliefs were playing so loud in my head that I hadn't really heard anything else. I finally understood that the only thing between me and my new dream was a false belief.

What would happen if you stopped believing that you can't have it, whatever *it* is for you?

There's an idea in Judaism that one of the first questions that God asks when you get to the heavenly gates is to answer for all the pleasure, all the goodness, and all the riches that were put into this world that you *denied* yourself. I find this question fascinating because it speaks directly to our beliefs about abundance and limitation, to our beliefs about self-worth and worthlessness—what we each believe we do and do not deserve. Do you believe you deserve abundance? Do you believe receiving an abundant life is your birthright? How did you answer the questions at the beginning of the chapter? Specifically, how did you respond to this one: Do you believe that abundance is reserved for *other people*? If your answer is "Yes, abundance is reserved for the lucky ones, the more deserving," you're not alone. Every day I meet people who question whether their hopes and dreams are possible. I meet people who feel depleted, burned out, resentful, and full of fear, who believe that abundance exists outside of them and is infinitely out of reach, and to this I say: You may believe that you are separate, that resources are limited, and scarcity is real, but the truth is there's enough for everyone because abundance isn't stuff. It's not stacks of cash. It's a free-flowing current, a frequency that's available to everyone, a frequency that's meant to circulate through our bodies and flow easily through our lives. And if you haven't felt or experienced this frequency yet, it's that you're tuned to the channel of limitation where your beliefs have created a limit, or a static barrier, to what you can receive.

This is why the ego doesn't really have a place in the manifesting conversation. When I ask people, "How much money would you love to manifest?" they'll say, "A million! A hundred grand! Ten billion!" The truth is that it really doesn't matter. It's all consciousness.

The real question is, how much consciousness would you allow yourself to receive? When I do this exercise with people, I'll then say, "All right, you wrote one million, you wrote ten billion. Now close your eyes. From the place of your soul, how much can you give? Is there a limit? And from the place of your soul? How much can you receive?"

The only answer is "endless." It's all available.

That's where most people realize, "Oh, this whole block I have against manifesting is because it's my ego." That's right—you don't get what you want. You get what you are.

TEST THE LIMIT

A few years ago, I gained a bunch of weight, basically out of nowhere. I watched my waist expand and my wardrobe change along with it. I wasn't sure why I was gaining weight, but my assistant had a theory. She said, "I hope I don't offend you, but based on some things I've heard you say, I think you've subconsciously gained weight because you want to be more relatable to people?"

"Huh?" I asked.

She continued, "Well, you're making millions of dollars now, you're very successful, and it seems like you're worried that your money will make you unrelatable to most people."

I stared at her dumbfounded, because what she said was 100 percent true, but I hadn't realized it. I did have a subconscious belief that making lots of money would make me unrelatable, unlikable, and as someone who really likes to be liked, I'd gone and gained a bunch of weight to appear more like a "regular" person. How ridiculous is that? Also, the more I thought about it, I realized that I believed that my financial success would set me apart from some of my best friends, as if my money meant I'd outgrown them and outgrown our friendship. So, what did I unconsciously do? I grew out of my own pants in an effort to keep my friends. Again, ridiculous. What was getting in the way of me being able to say to people, and especially some of my dearest friends, "I'm successful, I like my job, I love my husband, I have a cute Persian cat, three lovely daughters, and a nice sofa too." What was stopping me from openly acknowledging my success? I'll tell you—it was a false belief that success makes people unlikable, and a self-made woman who has earned a lot of money in a relatively short amount of time, and who's stayed mostly a size 6, is really unlikable. Am I wrong?

Well, yes, I was wrong, and once I became aware of this belief, this unconscious Muzak that kept me circling the refrigerator like a hungry bear, I dropped the seventeen pounds and while I was at it, I consciously dropped my limiting belief and replaced it with something new, one with a much higher vibe: I'm worthy and relatable just as I am. And what actually makes somebody relatable or not is their energy. When somebody's energy is loving, they're always relatable. It has nothing to do with appearance. It has nothing to do with what someone wears. You are relatable because you only know how to be loving and vulnerable and kind.

If you're coming up against this resistance yourself, you're not alone. Many women have been conditioned to access only a certain amount of their power every day. There's a fear that if we dug deeper and touched ground with the power within us, we would outgrow the people closest to us. We'd be so powerful, and what then? The thought of it can be so scary to women that they'll turn it off and dim their light. But the exciting thing is to turn it on and to allow yourself to rise into the person you know you're supposed to be.

The more abundance you have, the more abundance you create. If you plant a cherry tree for yourself, you know what you just did? You just created the opportunity for endless numbers of more cherry trees. The law of the universe is that abundance creates more abundance. When you are abundant, you don't take away someone else's ability to have abundance. You create it.

You're relatable just as you are.
For simply being you.

DITCH THE MUZAK!

Think about a belief that's limiting you. If you can't think of one, ask yourself: *In what area of my life do I feel limited, small, diminished, lacking?* For example, *I haven't received a work promotion in years* or *When it comes to parenting, I don't feel like my partner takes me seriously.* Once you have an unwanted situation, circumstance, or relationship in your mind, can you trace it back to a belief? This is akin to deconstructing a recipe to its essential ingredients. To help you break it down, take a look at the menu below. Do you recognize any of these beliefs as your own?

I'm not enough.

Things don't work out.

This is as good as it gets.

I'm not an expert at anything.

I'll always struggle.

Life is hard.

I'm not good with money.

Eventually, I'll lose it all.

People always leave me.

Nobody understands me.

I'll always be alone.

I don't have good ideas.

I don't matter.

I've wasted so much time.

I'm too old.

I'm insignificant.

My dreams are too big, too unrealistic.

I'm not ready.

I don't have enough resources.

No one will show up anyway.

Nobody comes through.

Who am I to do this?

Everyone will judge me.

The world is an unkind place.

The life I want is out of reach.

There's just no way it will ever happen.

Your beliefs create your reality, so take a second look at any of the beliefs above that ring true to or resonate with you. Most every woman I've ever coached sees themselves in at least one of them, if not several. And once they bravely identify the limiting belief that they're unconsciously humming along to, they wake up.

It's time for you to wake up. Are you listening?

One false belief like "I'm not ready" or "I don't matter" is a story that you're telling yourself about why the life of your dreams is not possible. Make no mistake: false beliefs like the ones listed above will undeniably affect your reality, like an echo, a boomerang, a hologram, a mirror image. Choose whatever metaphor you like and consider how your limiting beliefs are holding you apart from abundance.

How can a belief hold you back?

Beliefs hold an energetic vibration, so whatever you believe is energetically attuned to the life you're living. Once you understand that you've likely been falsely programmed by a set of passed-down beliefs that have been replaying in your subconscious mind for years, decades, *entire lifetime*, you can change the dial. For now, join me as I tune into the nature channel. Look no further than the unfolding leaves on a tree, the endless expanse of sand at the beach, the infinite waves that crash on the shore, and the stars in the night sky, and you cannot deny that limitless abundance surrounds us, every moment of the day. When you tune into the channel of the stars and change what you believe, you can begin living in a more expanded universe, one where you see—finally—the multitude of stars aligning in your life, the magnificent constellation that was already there, just waiting for you to look up and notice.

6.

SET YOURSELF APART FROM THE STATIC

EY, STARGAZER. Listen up: we've been talking a lot about the radio dial and now I want to mix it up because maybe you're not as obsessed with music as I am; maybe you're more of a visual learner, so allow me to introduce a new metaphor. You are not only the DJ of your life but also the director of the movie with the same title: *Your Life*. And as the director, you are managing what's in the spotlight by choosing where to focus your attention. This is amazing, creative power! You're in the director's chair—except for this: the recurring thoughts that create your beliefs direct the show. Now, this isn't necessarily a bad thing; in fact, it can work miracles in your favor. It can. But unfortunately, too many of us let our false beliefs lead the narrative and derail the unfolding plotline before we reach our happy ending.

As we talked about in the last chapter, we all have beliefs that were formed in our earliest years of life based on our environment and culture, our parents and caretakers, our friends and neighbors, our early schooling, and many other unique factors. These beliefs create a "cognitive bias"—a slanted way of thinking—that over time and without fail we confuse with the truth. Although, what's true is that our bias is only perception; it's how we've unconsciously programmed our own minds to *see* and make meaning of the world irrespective of what's actually going on. For example, you might sit down on a bench in your neighborhood park and feel uplifted by the sound of children laughing and playing on the swings. The person next to you might be feeling the heavy heart of deep grief because this was where they met their late father every Thursday afternoon, and the person on the end of the bench may hastily stand up and walk away because they find public parks to be dirty and "poor." Why are you three experiencing the same park so differently? Because each person's cognitive bias focuses in on a different aspect of the scene, like a single frame of a film. So many of us experience our lives like this, with a limited view, like we're wearing 3-D movie glasses that—have you ever noticed?—make it harder to see the movie. What I want to help you do is widen the aperture and see the whole picture—all of it—without blinders. I want to help you see all the potentials that already exist.

We don't truly see what *is* when we're trapped inside our mind.

BECOME CONSCIOUS OF YOUR UNCONSCIOUS

Did you know that for every second, there are four thousand pieces of information in front of you that you *won't* see because you have force-focused your experience? This isn't a "you" problem. We all do it, or at least, most all of us unconsciously sift through the information directly in front of us and look for evidence that will validate our cognitive bias. For example, have you ever been looking to buy a certain type of car and all of a sudden, Subaru Outbacks are the *only* cars you see on the road? Or you're pregnant, trying to get pregnant, or your best friend's pregnant and suddenly—poof!—pregnant women are everywhere! I'm not going to tell you that those pregnant women aren't real, that they're an illusion. They're absolutely real, and a lot of people drive Subarus. At the same time, there are other cars on the road and a lot of nonpregnant folks. You just didn't notice them because of your forced focus.

This is what's happening: Your mind is constantly organizing the world based on what you focus on. You walk into your life with a projector, like a movie projecting onto a screen, and you project that which is inside your mind. Then you reinforce that projection by finding evidence for everything that you project. That continues to get magnified, so you live it more and more and more. We always go first. The projector always goes first. This means you've already decided how that person meant what they said, you've already decided what this looks like or what it doesn't, you've already decided what's here or what's not possible. You will find the evidence and the data to support those projections, and you will get more of the same.

You are the director, and the great news is that you get to make whatever movie you want. You get to be in control of how this gets to feel and how expansive it gets to be. You don't have to worry about anything else, because it's constantly lining up. It's amazing.

When I had author Mike Dooley on my podcast, he said that we don't live in a neutral universe. It's net positive. The deck is so stacked in our favor that it's unbelievable. As soon as you start to play with this idea, to really believe in and look for evidence of it, you go, "Wow! Nineteen magical things just happened." That's because we're not playing with neutral. We're playing with such an aligned gift of positivity that as soon as you are a part of that stream and you take a step, immediately there's ten thousand steps coming around you from the universe. That is how powerful it is because energy collapses time and space.

If this is making your head spin, don't sweat it. Most of us aren't aware of our own perception, and becoming conscious of where you're unconscious is what I want to help you do, because when you become more aware of what you're focusing on and understand how to change your internal lens and broaden the frame, the movie of your life will become bigger and brighter, more colorful, more engaging, more like your favorite feel-good Rob Reiner movie. And because you are the director, this is 100 percent within your creative control. You just need some guidance, some script notes. And while I'd love to fast-forward to the part of the movie where you tap into abundance—we must still take a look at where you are now.

EVERY THOUGHT HAS A CHEMICAL REACTION

If you're like me, or most anyone on the planet, a single thought can ruin your whole day. *Am I in the right marriage? Am I in the wrong career? Why did I say "yes" when I meant "no"? Why do I always feel different and alone?* These types of negative thoughts can give me a regret hangover that lasts not only a full day but an entire week. I said earlier that for every second, there are four thousand pieces of information being presented to us. Well, over the course of a single day, we have seventy thousand individual thoughts, and for most of us, those thoughts are negatively biased. Stop and think about that—seventy thousand thoughts a day that are predominantly negative. What a tragedy, and this is precisely why so many of us, irrespective of our professions, education, politics, age, geography, or religion, get caught in the illusion of scarcity and separation: *I am not enough. I don't do enough. I don't have enough. I will never be enough.* Negative thoughts don't just derail our sense of self; they also have a chemical effect that goes like this: when you think something that leaves you feeling anxious or upset, your brain releases cortisol, the stress hormone.

On top of that, cortisol has an addictive quality. It's hungry. In fact, it's more addictive than nicotine, so as soon as it's released into our cells, our bodies crave more of it, and for those of us on a regular diet of negativity, the addiction is relentless. We can become addicted to feeling bad. Just one negative thought can be all it takes to derail us, to make negativity multiply, triggering more cortisol production like a pharmaceutical drip in your brain and continuing the cycle. During this state of stress, anxiety, overwhelm, or negativity, our cells are not repairing. For example, when a woman is stressed out, sometimes she'll skip a period because the body says, "Uh oh, this isn't a good place to create." The body cannot focus on creating because it is struggling just to survive.

In order to create, we need to be safe. We need to be at ease. That's when we're allowed to move into that next dimension. We'll then start to hear and perceive a way bigger aperture, a way bigger lens. It's always here; we just don't see it. This is why it's so important to tune into how regulated we are every single day. Once we have a bedrock of peace, then we're available to expand and we're available for creation.

My friend Kate Northrup shared this powerful process to calm the nervous system:

1. Stop.
Notice the signs that you are dysregulated. Recognize that "I don't feel safe. I'm dysregulated. It's not that I need to find a new strategy to grow my business or to make more money. It's actually that I just don't feel safe because something's going on."

2. Signal safety.
There are many ways to do this, but here's one example Kate shared. Notice gravity. If you're sitting on a chair, notice what it feels like to sit on the chair. Notice that gravity is just there for you. If you're standing, feel your

feet on the ground. Feel how gravity is holding you on the surface of the earth. You don't have to do anything to earn that. You don't have to do a thing to keep it from happening. It's just happening. Here in this moment, we are safe. Noticing gravity and how it feels on the body is a great way to signal safety.

When you're first implementing this practice, you can't have the expectation that it'll immediately stop a panic attack, but it'll help you slow it down a few degrees. As you repeat this over time, these things can work very quickly.

3. Solve.
Our innate tendency is to be dysregulated and automatically try to solve the problem. But when we solve a problem from a place of lack of safety, the solution we create will only perpetuate a dysregulated state. Our culture and our minds are designed that way. So it's a revolutionary act to learn to feel safe inside yourself, no matter what is going on outside. This is the ultimate move. And that is plugging you into Source, whatever divine power that is for you. Once we connect to Source, then we solve. The truth is, often there's not really a problem to begin with. It's just what our bodies signaled to us.

When you think something bad, you don't feel good.

I'll share how my own addiction to cortisol plays out in my life. On any given day, I wake up feeling pretty good (this is a practice I've cultivated and that I'll share with you soon), but by late morning, I will unconsciously go looking for something to feel bad about—questioning whether I'm making the right choice about where to live or something my husband said twelve years ago. Frustration, guilt, fear, regret—suddenly the cortisol kicks in and I cannot resist feeling bad. Recently, a series of negative thoughts threatened to escalate and multiply. It happened after my family moved into our gorgeous new home, the home of my dreams, and one I worked hard to achieve. We'd been in the house for only one week when I began to think, *Do I really deserve this? Who do I think I am? Maybe I should move out?* Crazy thoughts, I'm telling you, and it was my negativity at the door, begging me to let it in. I was tempted, I really was, until my awareness saved the day. My awareness elbowed its way to the forefront of my mind and reminded me: those negative thoughts at work are just thoughts, and just because you think them doesn't make them true. The choice is yours: you can choose to feed them or starve them.

WHY FEED THE BEAST?

We feed ourselves negative thoughts because it's our habit; often, we don't know or remember what our life feels like *without* this self-sabotaging habit. We don't know what it feels like to feel better. The great news is that we have the capacity to shift and change our bad habits, to Ctrl + Alt + Delete the way we've been thinking unconsciously for years, sometimes over our entire lifetimes. There's evidence that the happiest people in the world are those who have broken from their cortisol addiction. My friend and author Dan Buettner, who wrote *Blue Zones* and hosted the brilliant Netflix series *Live to 100: Secrets of the Blue Zones*, shines a spotlight on geographical pockets around the world where people are happier because they're more aware of their thoughts and what they allow themselves to believe, and as a result of their healthy mental diet, their brains release more serotonin and dopamine, the feel-good hormones, into their system. This is a significant part of their lifestyle that causes them to live past one hundred years because they have substantially less cortisol.

GROW YOUR AWARENESS IN THE MOMENT

Where am I right now? Am I feeling dysregulated, or do I feel at ease in my body? Where is my focus? One of the most powerful practices you can start today is to notice what you're feeling and how it impacts your thoughts. Again, this sounds so simple, except most of us aren't usually aware of our thought patterns; we let them float into our minds and bodies and accept them without question, even though—a lot of the time—they're fake news. My mindfulness teacher used to say: if you walked into your home late at night and the house lights were not on, you would not stub your toe on the staircase because you know the layout of your own house; you've walked through it countless times. But if you left a key under the mat for a guest staying at your house who returned home late at night and the lights were not on, the person would likely bump into a door and step into the dog dish. Moral of the story: when you're aware of your thoughts, you are less likely to lose your way, even in the dark.

CLEAR OUT THE EMOTIONAL CONGESTION

I had a conversation with my friend Tracy Litt, an author and teacher of spirituality and the manifestation mindset. She said that earlier in her life, she had constant dysregulation that was creating emotional congestion. And this was blocking her from the ability to have an authentic frequency, which also caused her to feel terrible every day. She said, "Unprocessed emotion is the most detrimental thing in your experience, period. The truth about emotion is that it's energy in motion. This is a highly conscious definition and understanding of emotion. We've been led to believe that emotion is good or bad, high or low. That judgment of emotion is what makes us suppress tears or think we have to suck it up."

She said, "We add to that having mothers and grandmothers that weren't ever liberated to express themselves and feel their feelings. You never saw them in a mode where they would excuse themselves from the table and go to the closet, or cry in the bathroom. All of these things add up to the point when you realize that *No one taught me that it was safe to be expressive.* And you cannot be the fullest expression of who you are if you are suppressed, repressed, oppressed, and depressed on an emotional level.

"Emotional congestion—those emotions that haven't been processed—don't miraculously clear out of your body while you're sleeping. They get stuck, and stay inside your system until you become a woman who expresses, which means feeling it until it's done being felt without judgment. That's how we each get to authentic frequency."

Tracy has a four-step process to cultivate the nonjudgmental observer version of yourself. She said it must be nonjudgmental "because if you're in judgment, you're in the third dimension of consciousness. And that's like trying to grow while you're standing in quicksand. It's never gonna happen."

Notice what emotional state you're in.

Make it safe. Go from dysregulation into regulation. This could be grounding yourself in the grass, shaking your body out, employing deep breathing patterns, taking a bath, or even doing a few reps of some intense exercise. You get whatever is in your system out and you move yourself into a regulated state.

Once you become regulated, your prefrontal cortex comes back online, which is your ability to consciously choose. Next, ask yourself, "What would she do?" The "she" is the woman you're becoming. When you leave your current identity, she's going to give you a beautiful, highly conscious, loving answer, because she's the version of you that's already marinating and living and waking up every day in your dream. She's already living in that potential.

You do what she says. If she says, regulate some more, you honor that. If she says, pick up the phone and make the phone call, you honor that. If she says go hug them right now, you honor that. If she says let the team member go, you honor that. Trust is critical. Embrace it and let her lead.

STOP, NOTICE, AND QUESTION

Take a moment now. Check in for ninety seconds.

Close your eyes and ask yourself, "Is my nervous system regulated? Or is it feeling uneasy?" Either way, there's no judgment. Next, ask yourself, "How do I find my Self here? Where is my soul? Where is she? There she is. What does she need me to know today?"

Don't push for an answer. Maybe you'll get one. Maybe you won't.

Then ask yourself, "What do I want to feel today? I'm going to select my feelings the way I select my thoughts, the way I select my clothes. What would ease feel like today? Try it on. What would joy feel like?" Pick one. Then for the rest of that ninety seconds, feel what that feels like. Feel it in your body.

Once you open your eyes, ask yourself, "Okay, what's the one thing I now feel like doing? To whom would I speak? What would I say? What would I post? What would I create? Maybe what I feel like doing right now is to simply nourish myself."

This practice only takes a minute and a half, but it can change your whole life because you'll have your own attention. When you have your own attention, you won't lose the whole day being unconscious and repeating the thoughts and feelings you had yesterday.

WHEN MY BODY gives rise to an unpleasant feeling, like that escalating anxiety I talked about earlier, I *stop* and consciously notice the thought behind it: Who do I think I am to move into a house like this? I don't deserve it. Typically, when we feel bad, it's because our thoughts are working against us, sending us junk mail. So, once you identify the thought, question the thought. I love Byron Katie's method of self-inquiry that encourages us to put a question mark at the end of every thought. *Is this thought true?* And if the thought's not true, replace it with the truth. Sometimes easier said than done. If you're not sure if the thought is true or false, set it aside for later. For example—

Who do I think I am to move into a house like this? I don't deserve it. Maybe I should find another place.

Is this thought true?

Is it absolutely beyond a shadow of a doubt the truth?

What is the actual truth?

Since we learn through repetition, I'm going to say this again. *In this life, we don't get what we want; we get what we are.* We get what we *are*, so to reprogram yourself, to create change, the internal work is to cultivate awareness. This chapter is about attuning yourself to *What am I thinking? What do I believe? How do these thoughts and beliefs make me feel?* And, by extension, *How do they influence my reactions and how I show up in this world?* Remember, your brain is hardwired into an automatic program that's been running since you were very young and you've been unconsciously repeating those subconscious beliefs—*I am not enough, I am not deserving, I am not safe, I am not lovable*—which are not facts; they're just thoughts you've been thinking on automatic. And because those thoughts are likely to be steeped in limitation, scarcity, fear, and lack, when you think them, you feel bad. And what happens when we feel bad? Our body releases cortisol, which keeps us in a fearful, anxious state. This cycle of feeling limited and that the life we desire is not available keeps us stuck, frustrated, exhausted, and pissed off—am I right?

Of course, none of us mean to stay stuck but we will not and cannot move forward until we stop the old program and upgrade our beliefs to align with a higher frequency that directs us forward, *finally*, toward abundance. This takes work and practice, and it is doable, and one of the ways to do this is to question the beliefs that make us feel bad: *Is this really true? Why do I believe this? What is true? What thoughts can I choose to have that are closer to the truth?* To be clear, I'm not suggesting that you dissect every thought that crosses your mind—gosh, how exhausting!—no, what I'm encouraging you to do is to cultivate an inner awareness of your cognitive bias—where you are perceiving yourself, your circumstances, or your life negativity so that you're no longer stumbling around in the dark, unconscious of how your thoughts are influencing your reality.

PRESENCE: THE ANTIDOTE TO CORTISOL

Okay, so now you're becoming more aware of your thoughts, you're loving yourself with your new level awareness, and—then, what?

Get curious about meditation.

When I tell my students that the skeleton key to the chocolate factory is some kind of meditation practice, they often resist—no, not that!—so, if you have a similar resistance to meditation, you're not alone. And I get it. The good news is that you don't have to have a strict meditation practice to get the benefits of meditation.

Meditation, as I define it, is focused attention without judgment. It is not the act of stopping the mind; it's cultivating a relationship with the mind. Which means you are allowed to think during meditation; it's just a different kind of thinking. It leans heavily into inquiry, curiosity, witnessing, and observation. It accepts what comes into the mind without judgment, kind of like, *Huh, there's that thought again. I wonder what that's about.* When we become a witness to our thoughts, we snap into the present moment, and—lo and behold—that's meditating.

I talked to neuroscientist Dr. Amishi Jha and she said our attention is constantly being pulled in a million different places. There's so much stimulation. You've got all these notifications on your phone, you've got work, you've got your kids. We've created this culture where there's not a lot of pausing. There's not a lot of attention on this moment.

Dr. Jha said that with a mindfulness practice, we can direct our attention like a flashlight. We can point that flashlight and intentionally choose where to focus our attention. So no matter what moment you're in—whether you're sitting in traffic or you're reading a book or your plans just got canceled or you're trying on a pair of jeans—you can choose to take the flashlight and focus on this present moment. You can come right back into this moment, and then you might notice that there's 149 shades of green outside. You might notice that it feels good to be here and that there's no other moment you need to get to that holds your well-being. You notice there's an equanimity, there's peace.

Nobody can take your vibration from you. No one. You're the creator of your capacity to receive, period. It's where you put your focus. It's where your energy is. It's where your attention is. It's how far you can see. It's how much you can hold. And our environment can't take that away from us. In fact, that's how powerful we are. When our energy is aligned, we influence the environment, and not the other way around.

A fancier way to say this is that when we become a witness to our thoughts, we are entering *witness consciousness*; we are actively engaging in the present moment. In this space, we recognize that we have thoughts, we have a relationship to them, but we are not our thoughts.

Did you get that? We *have* thoughts. We are not our thoughts.

In fact, we are each much bigger than our thoughts. We have a mind beyond our mind, a consciousness that connects us to the *highest* frequency in the universe. This sounds incredible because it is, and we can *know* this, we can each *feel* this through meditation, through focused attention and awareness without judgment. I know, for someone who hated her first experience meditating, I'm selling it hard—and that's because I've experienced this internal shift and, as a result, I've seen so many incredible things show up in my life that go far beyond financial wealth, and I want you to experience this too. The more you meditate, the more you will become a witness to your negative thoughts, and when you begin to separate the negative mind chatter from your consciousness—the fake news from the truth—that's when the magic happens. Meditation becomes a tool that can not only help you separate yourself from your most negative thoughts but also connect you to that higher frequency where your abundance is waiting for you. Meditation can lead to more connection with others, higher insights, big ideas, and greater capacity for creation and transformation.

When we have this recognition that we are not defined by our feelings or our thoughts, that's when we can learn how to be with them. My mindfulness teacher used to say that it's like having tea with yourself every morning and inviting every part of you to join. Every aspect is welcome—the part of you that is brave and fierce, the part of you that's a liar, the part that self-sabotages, and the part that is wise and loving. Every part is welcome at the table every morning. That is how we find wholeness and equanimity. That is how we find well-being and coherence. Instead of walking around with shame, we become a witness to all that is, and in so doing we feel at ease.

Through meditation I learned that we're a lot like the ocean. Most of the time, we associate the ocean with the waves. Depending on the day, you might describe the waves as frenetic or choppy or crashing. Even on a calm day, the waves are constant, always moving, always making sound. But here's the thing—the waves are the most superficial part of the ocean. They're the surface-level chatter. Anyone who's spent time on the water knows how deep and how vast the ocean truly is. And what happens when you dive down ten feet, fifty feet, a mile? It's so serene and so quiet that the stillness can burst your ears. In reality, the ocean should be characterized by its stillness. Our minds are like the waves, always moving, but within us is this deep quiet, like the ocean itself.

On my podcast, I've interviewed more than nine hundred of the smartest, most interesting people, and I can tell you that the one thing that's most consistent among them all is having a meditation practice. Why? Because these individuals understand that there are no true answers in the choppy waters of the mind. The biggest insights and creative downloads and clear directives forward exist at a deeper level, in the beyond mind, in our greater consciousness.

I talked with author and entrepreneur Gino Wickman, who said, "Be aware of your thoughts, emotions, feelings, and decisions as they come up throughout the day. And just start to realize which ones are coming from fear, which ones are coming from love. It's just about being aware. And that's why stillness practices like meditation, journaling, prayer, and contemplation are wonderful forms that allow you to sit in silence and let it all come up. A lot of us fear sitting in silence because that's when stuff wants to come up. Allow it anyway, allow it to move through."

I completely understood what he was talking about. In the past year I'd gone to a week-long retreat in Vail, Colorado, with Dr. Joe Dispenza. I had been to his retreats before, but this one was with a much smaller group, and it was much more intense than what we had done in the past. I could feel that I was fighting myself, and all these thoughts popped up like, *Who does he think he is? This is pointless.* But it had nothing to do with him. It's just that the act of sitting in silence gave room for those thoughts to appear.

But after I broke through, I had the most beautiful encounter of my life. I wound up seeing all the thoughts of love that had been sent toward me by all the wonderful people in my life. It felt as if there were an escrow account of all this love that had been waiting for me. And it took me to my knees. I realized, *Oh my God, there is an escrow account of LOVE available to me right now.* I could feel all the prayer that my husband had sent up for me, my grandparents, all this love. I was completely taken into the most essential part of myself. It was one of the most powerful and humbling moments of my life.

As scary as it is to sit with yourself, the payoff is magnificent. Even though I always try to come up with some excuse to not meditate or attend these long retreats, I push myself to do it because I know I'll come back having completely changed the radio dial inside myself. It's such a needed reset so I can hear different music.

Now, if you're still thinking meditation isn't for you, trust me, everyone can do it, and people whom you may not suspect are doing it. Jerry Seinfeld starts his day with meditation. Oprah is a big proponent of meditation. Steve Jobs was deep into it, and when Phil Jackson coached the Los Angeles Lakers and the Chicago Bulls, he had all his players meditate regularly. And guess what? The Bulls won six NBA championships under his leadership and the Lakers won three. Yes, talent played into those wins, no doubt, and also—I guarantee you—a meditative mindset made the game.

And just as there's not a "type" of person who meditates, there's also no one way to do it. In my workshops, people will frequently say—"I'm doing it all wrong. My mind won't stop."

Just as the ocean's waves don't stop, neither will your mind. As I said earlier, the point isn't to stop your thoughts. The point is to change your relationship to them and to drop into the part of you that is your wise, essential self beyond the mind. It's the consciousness and intuition that is always available to you. It's always a breath away. "How" you do that is really up to you. There are several ways that are easy and effective. I go on meditation retreats a few times a year, and every day I meditate in any number of ways. In between recording podcasts or writing, I may take a few quiet moments to sit in the sun and savor the cool breeze. I often take a walk through my neighborhood before picking the kids up from school and remember to take off my shoes and walk in the grass for a few moments. Some days I listen to a visualization app on my phone or a guided meditation on YouTube over my first cup of coffee. Whatever I do, the intention is the same—tap into that inner stillness.

USING MEDITATION TO TUNE IN

I had a beautiful conversation with meditation teacher Thomas Hubl about the power of presence and attunement, which he defines as the essence of relating. He said that our presence in life shows itself in every moment; therefore, there's no moment that's more or less important. They're all part of presence. When you're stressed, you can't enjoy the small moments that reveal the state of your nervous system. He said that's why "meditation for many people is also difficult because it's not about the thinking mind. The thinking mind is just a symptom of a stressed nervous system that creates all these thought processes. So, when we want to come into our mind, we actually need to down regulate the stress in our body." We need to be attuned to ourselves. We need to be that witness to ourselves. When we do this, we can be with what is. When you feel the flow of who you are, you connect with your self-worth because you understand that you don't need some external thing to tell you if you're good or not.

When we enter that meditative state, we're reminded that there's so much peace and freedom there. We're reminded that the old part of our reptilian brain is always chasing the high; it's always chasing more. But our conscious self is chasing equanimity. It's searching for the moments in between the highs and lows.

Picture that you're sitting beside a river and the stream is going at whatever pace it's going. There's no need to force it. Just be with it as it is. Feel into how delicious it is to just be present, sitting beside the river—not pushing the river, not chasing. Just being present. There's something so gratifying about being in these ordinary extraordinary moments. You'll come to realize that the beauty of it is even better than the highs that we're chasing.

Rehearse for a New Line

Meditation is a tool to help you become conscious of where you've been unconscious, so that you can begin to choose more thoughts that align with abundance. Just as we choose our clothes every day, we can each become mindful of choosing our thoughts. Every morning, we each have a choice—we can allow our minds to spin, to be tempted by our cortisol addiction that craves negativity, or we can shift the dial by choosing to think differently. I said earlier that most mornings I wake up feeling pretty good, and that's due to a practice I've built like a muscle. There's a morning prayer we recite in Jewish tradition called Modeh Ani. It's a beautiful practice of saying thank you to the divine for giving us another day. The second half of the prayer reminds us that our soul is needed to contribute to the world, and every day that we're here is a reminder that we have a meaningful role to play on behalf of the collective. After I wake up and as I'm lying in bed, before turning on the light or even saying hello to my husband, I remember to express gratitude for the day, and consider the ways in which I will contribute to it. Then I select my thoughts and feelings for the day. I ask myself, "What would ease feel like today? What would joy and surrender feel like today?" Then I practice feeling that feeling for ninety seconds. It changes the trajectory of my whole day.

Reach a Boiling Point

I wish it were, but it's just not enough to dip into meditation once in a while or repeat a new lyric when you're stuck in the carpool lane. The unfortunate truth is that most of the time, when people begin a practice of shifting their energy, they give up almost as soon as they start because most of us have a negativity bias that whispers in our ear, *This will never work.*

To become a receiver of abundance, of the bright vision you have for yourself, not only do you have to silence those unhelpful thoughts but you also ought to work as hard as you can to reach a high vibration and *stay there*. Esther Hicks, inspirational speaker and author, describes this process in terms of boiling water, and it goes something like this: Vibration is like boiling water. Before a kettle of water boils, it's just water, but if I put the kettle on the stove and turn on the heat, what happens? It boils. Does it boil the second that I turn on the heat? No, it takes some time to heat up, and if I leave the kettle on the stove, it will eventually boil. Every time. It's that consistent. But what do most people do? They turn the heat off before the water comes to a boil. They become impatient with waiting. Some may even convince themselves that it's not going to boil, ever. It's typically this same group of folks who keep opening the oven while it's preheating to impatiently conclude, *It's not heating up!* For water to boil, for the oven to heat, and for you to raise your vibration, the instructions are the same: Wait. Stick with it. Don't walk away or turn the heat off. Allow your inner temperature to rise, and with practice, patience, and persistence, it will *get there*.

> Focus on your vibration,
> focus on your temperature rising,
> and with the consistency of boiling water,
> it will rise.

FLOW READY

I asked mindfulness coach George Mumford what it was like to work with Phil Jackson and the Chicago Bulls and the Los Angeles Lakers, and how meditation and mindfulness gave players their edge.

He said, "Wisdom begins in wonder, and this is the idea of being in the zone. Joseph Campbell talked about an element that's really important—that when an athlete is at championship form, they're coming out of this place of rest. I call it the eye of the hurricane. And when they come out of that, when they're in championship form, they're performing from the 'eye,' not being driven by fear or desire but holding their center. And then at some point, you catch the current and it just carries you. There's no self-consciousness. You're not worried about how you're doing. You have supreme confidence and there's a premonition aspect that takes over where you see things happening before they happen, because you're relating on another level where there's no ego. You got out of the way so that you can just express yourself honestly."

LIFE SAVERS

Another powerful conversation I had on the podcast was with author Hal Elrod who wrote *The Miracle Morning,* an incredible book about six timeless, proven personal-development practices that the world's most successful people have sworn by for centuries. He organized them into the acronym SAVERS:

S (silence): any kind of meditative practice you can do
A (affirmations)
V (visualizations)
E (exercise): doesn't have to be a crazy workout, but any movement
R (reading)
S (scribing): journaling or writing

He said, "How you start your day sets the tone, the context, and the direction for how you show up to the rest of your day. If you win the morning, you are in a peak position to win the day. These six practices will benefit you anytime of day, but when you do them in the morning, you're putting yourself in a peak physical, mental, emotional, and spiritual state. And then you get to take on every aspect of your day as the best version of yourself, as a better version of who went to bed the night before."

He attributes SAVERS to saving his life when he was diagnosed with a rare form of cancer and was given only a 20–30 percent chance of survival. All six of his SAVERS at that time were focused on his outcome of beating cancer—and his commitment to having this practice every morning literally saved his life.

What if doing nothing was the most productive use of your time?

Just yesterday, after I recorded a podcast and worked on this book, it started to rain, the kind of rain that comes down in sheets and relieves the air of all its heaviness. For about thirty minutes, I sat out on my balcony and listened to it. At first, I thought I should bring out my phone or a book to read, and I intentionally stopped myself. I asked, *What if, instead, I did nothing? What if I just sat still and listened to the rain? How epic would that be? To enjoy the quiet and allow myself to remember that I am more than a podcaster, a writer, a mom, a wife.* In this moment of spontaneous self-reflection, I felt myself connecting . . . I am connected to the *highest* frequency on the radio dial. I am a creative being.

ONE NOTE AT A TIME

It took me years to have a consistent mindfulness practice, but almost as soon as I started introducing activities like meditation and taking more walks, spending time in nature by getting outside in the middle of the day

for ten minutes, long enough to feel the sun hit my face or feel the grass between my toes, I experienced a shift. The type of shift where you realize how
each moment holds a special kind of fullness where there's nothing to pull,
there's nothing to force or push, and where you feel like *I'm in the right place
in the right time.* That's what presence is: being right here, right now.

When I allow myself to show up in the present moment, I receive not
only a greater sense of ease and peace but also my biggest creative downloads. When I show up in the right place and at the right time, unexpected
and wonderful opportunities are waiting—right there—for me to stop and
notice them. When we slow down and pause in between the notes, we connect to the *highest* frequency on the radio dial where anything is possible,
but for us to really hear all the possibilities that are playing, we must be
tuned in; we must hold space to listen.

BE MORE. DO LESS.

What if doing nothing was the most productive use of your time? Let's build
on that: what if doing something "unproductive" led to your next creative
idea? In the days and weeks ahead, continue to challenge yourself to make
time and space to be unproductive. To just be. To create space between the
notes. This could be a half hour coloring after the kids go to bed or grabbing
their Play-Doh and joining in their fun. Maybe it's baking something sweet
or arranging cut flowers from your garden. Arguably, these activities aren't
unproductive; they serve to help us show up to the present moment, which
is what I call creative productivity. When I interviewed psychologist Mike
Rucker, author of *The Fun Habit*, he said when you spend two hours of your
day doing things without there needing to be a result, when you do things
just because they feel good to do them, by the time you go back to "work,"

you're more efficient, more potent, and more productive. For all you over-achievers reading this, I hope that gives you incentive to play more. To slow down. To unplug and underproduce. It's in this space that we tap into our creative reserves, and from there—BOOM! Anything's possible.

And before you tell me, "Sorry, Cathy, life is so busy, and the daily grind takes over. I don't have time for creativity and play," let me ask you this question: How much time do you spend a day on your phone? Come clean. Really, be honest. When I pose this question in retreats, I tend to receive pushback. Most people don't want to give me their phone. I mean, they *really* don't want to give me their phone. They clutch it tight and insist that they're busy, that they have a full plate, and that the phone is not to blame. So I push back harder: "Come on, give me that phone. Just give me that phone. I want to see your screen time tracker." Eventually, they relent and it's a sobering ex-ercise because guess how much time a day, on average, most people spend on their phones? Three to six hours. That's the equivalent of a part-time job. Imagine if you gave yourself half of that time to allow for creative thought. What might be possible? Our culture doesn't advocate time to just *be*. And many of us, whether we admit it or not, are afraid of empty space. For some, it feels lonely. Scary, even. For others, it feels idle and boring. But here's the juicy secret: empty space allows for creative flow, and there's nothing lonely, scary, or boring about that.

In our being, we are our most creative.

Tapping into abundance is about learning to become that tuning fork. This is why every morning, to manifest a beautiful new reality, I take a mo-ment to breathe and meditate. I start by dropping into the gratitude for all the fullness and beauty in my life. I then focus on widening my perspective to perceive a greater expansive view of this world. I feel that I am not a body, not bound by time or space. I am connected to the part of me that is floating in the timeless vast energy of the whole universe, and that is where all potentials exist. The truth is, you already have everything you need within your essential self. So, when people say, "I desire X, Y, and Z," they're pushing it away. The thing you want most—when you crave it the most, when you long for it the most—the deeper the craving, the deeper the longing, the further away it is. When there's a feeling of lack and the absence of what is, that absence is what you create. But when there's wholeness, you can create that too. The more you feel the feelings of deep gratitude, of awe, of wonder, the more you can't help but bump into this amazing reality all the time.

WHATEVER WE TELL OURSELVES, our minds will begin to search for evidence that it's true, not just in the moment but throughout the day. Interestingly, research has shown that when we say something we don't believe is true, it activates and reinforces what we do believe is true. For example, if you wake up and say, "Abundance is available for me today; I live a life of ease and joy," but what you truly believe is that abundance is out of reach, then despite what you say, your beliefs will activate the energy of limitation. So what can you do? The most powerful work-around that I've found is to reframe your affirmation to match your belief *more closely*. Here are a couple examples using the "I experience abundance and ease every single day" affirmation in a situation where you do not believe that abundance is something you can or deserve to have . . . yet.

> *Add "What if" to the beginning:* "What if it does work out? What if more well-being is available every single day?"
> *Add "I am beginning to":* "I am beginning to allow more blessings into my life with ease."

When you reframe your intentions in this way, the mind doesn't tend to push back and object with "That's not true" or "Yeah, right." It allows for the possibility.

Try it.

Rehearse a new line that feels believable to you, or holds the truth of possibility, and notice how you feel. Do you feel a willingness to allow it? Permission to receive it? Notice if you experience an energetic uptick when you repeat these new thoughts out loud.

Creating a daily habit of rehearsing new lines is important because we learn through repetition. That's how we all learned the alphabet; that's how we learned our times tables. In fact, there's a method to what can feel like madness. As it relates directly to receiving abundance, we receive at the speed of safety. What does that mean? For us to increase our capacity for more freedom, connection, ease, meaning, and joy in our lives, we must feel safe in our nervous system. We simply cannot receive when our bodies are dysregulated, so the beauty of rehearsing new lines and repeating affirmations is that the repetition has a calming effect. It lowers our cortisol levels—our fight-or-flight-or-freeze responses—and shifts us into a state of allowing. Also, in order to have more, we have to create room for more, right? And this is what rehearsing new lines achieves. It aligns your energy with what is possible, and it brings your awareness to the present moment, giving you control over the moment that you don't always realize you have. As with meditation, build this habit into your day; over time, these new lines will replace the old ones. Your limiting beliefs and cognitive biases will be replaced with a new script, one that reflects a new focus and a bigger picture for your life.

7.

PLEASE YOURSELF

AUTHENTICITY VERSUS BELONGING

Too many women believe we must abandon ourselves in subtle ways and big ways in order to make everyone okay. We think it's our job to give, to put ourselves last, and, by all means, to be pleasing. Once I was at lunch with a friend, and through the window of the restaurant I watched as my car got a parking ticket. I didn't make a move; I continued sitting and watching because I was too concerned that leaving the conversation would hurt my friend's feelings. We believe that these are acts of generosity. My friend Mark Groves sees this differently. He says that all day long, most people make a choice between authenticity and belonging, and most of us choose belonging. A sense of belonging is delicious, it's a wonderful place to be, *but*—the trouble with choosing belonging over authenticity means you'll never belong to yourself. The quest to belong to others is an exhausting exercise in self-editing. When you edit yourself to belong to someone else or to a group of people, guess what? You stop belonging to yourself. And boy, what a lonely and unsafe place that is to be, and one that inevitably leads to great suffering because when we don't belong to ourselves, we don't really belong to anyone.

We live our lives with this constant second-guessing: *What will they think about me? What will they say?* We don't want to be judged or disliked or called a nasty word. The truth is people are way too busy being self-absorbed to really spend more than fifteen seconds thinking about you. Sure, they might unfollow or make a passing comment about you, but within five minutes something much juicier becomes their point of focus.

It's incredible how many of our decisions are made by the tally of everyone else's votes rather than just letting our own truth be enough to decide what is best.

So dye your hair purple, quit your job if you want to, tell the truth about how you actually feel, and be sure as hell certain that when you get to eighty-eight years old you can look back and say you lived *your* life rather than the life that pleased other people.

Take a stand. Pick a side. Be bold. Eat the last piece of cake. It's your one and only effing life.

Nobody cares in the end except for you, and the thing you'll care more about is leaving this world knowing you didn't miss the thrill of being who you were created to be. Here's a liberating notion: there are already people who don't like you. There are plenty of people you don't care for. That's okay. You can free yourself from being everyone's favorite and just focus on being your own.

**If we belong to everyone,
we cannot belong to ourselves.**

Because of my work, I meet women desperate to belong and to feel accepted, and who outsource their self-confidence to others. They show up in my workshops and I can visibly see the suffering and exhaustion they carry from wanting to guarantee a green light, the affirmative signal that someone is cosigning approval of them. And while they may get it, in their attempt to control the criticism, judgment, or nasty comments from others, they abandon their authentic selves.

Don't do this. It's not worth it. And it's unnecessary.

As my friend Susie Moore says, "The problem is not that people don't like you. The problem is that you think it's a problem." It's just a fact of life, and we need to accept it, allow it, and move on. There are people right now who don't like you and you're surviving it. There are people who are threatened by you, who don't like the decisions you make, who would rather not spend time with you. These people exist. Some might be living on your block. Others might be in your own family.

So what?

This is not a *you* problem. Because it isn't about you. It really isn't. The story that others project onto you is more about them. Their projection. Their perception. And that's not yours to control. And furthermore—there are people *you* don't like. There are people who aren't your cup of tea, and that's okay, isn't it? Do we all have to like the same things? I love sushi, Jerry Seinfeld, and Sour Patch Kids, and there are plenty of people who do not like any of those things. That's okay by me. Is it okay with you?

STOP REACTING

So many women I talk to share with me their belief that if somebody rejects them or is rude to them, if someone doesn't agree with their opinion or questions their decisions, then they believe they've done something egregiously wrong. And what I tell them is that what's wrong is believing that someone else's reaction is yours. Let me say it a different way: how people react to you is their reaction, their responsibility. And how much more freedom would you have if you stopped reacting to how others are reacting to you? What would it feel like to stop worrying about external approval, to belong to others, and to simply show up in the world as *you*?

Too risky? Too scary? Too potentially displeasing?

How about the converse: Freeing! Liberating!

Bronnie Ware, the author of the international bestseller *The Top Five Regrets of Dying*, was on my podcast, and she shared that the number-one regret of the dying was not living life on their own terms. Instead, they'd lived the life that others wanted for them or projected onto them. Heavy, right? And not a mistake any of us ought to make.

> Imagine living a life on your own terms.
> How would it look and feel different
> from the one you're living now?

The simple truth is that we were not designed to be all things to everyone. We were each designed to be authentic, unapologetically true to ourselves.

RECOVERING PEOPLE PLEASER

The dynamic in my house growing up was unpredictable and tense. I trained myself to read the temperature of the room, to anticipate when my parents' arguments might escalate. I learned to be hypervigilant and to overfunction in order to feel safe. I would listen to their complaints about each other and their unhappy lives, to be the good daughter who tried to help. I didn't realize then that in an effort to feel safe and to feel that I *belonged*, I created a codependency on people-pleasing. I used to think codependency related only to a dependency on other people, and I have since learned that we can be codependent on our desire for approval, on our need to belong, and this co-dependency drives us away from our own authenticity. It turns off our radio. In other words, we cannot receive an abundant life when we're not tuned into ourselves. My reaction to my home life was to turn myself into a pretzel to manage the temperature in the house, always be helpful, and have no needs. I learned to be someone other than Cathy. I lost myself until I finally *remembered* that pleasing everyone is not why I am here.

So many of us have lost ourselves. We no longer know where we end and the other person begins because we're so accustomed to pleasing. And we live in fear, afraid of displeasing others to the point that we say "yes" when our heart is telling us "no." Too many of us don't step forward and ask for what we need and desire because we don't want to be perceived as selfish. I've met women who believe they're acting generously by sidestepping their own needs to avoid triggering, offending, or potentially hurting someone else. Do you do that too? Have you ever had a clear opinion that you kept to yourself for fear of what others might say in return if you said it out loud? I get it. I've been there, but when you go to great lengths to belong and get along, you're ultimately abandoning yourself. Pleasing is exhausting work, and I won't speak for you, but I have to ask—aren't you tired of it?

I DON'T NEED PERMISSION TO BE ACKNOWLEDGED

Consider the following question: Where in my life am I showing up in a people-pleasing way? In what environments and with what people am I codependent on approval? Do I seek approval from my spouse or partner? Do I feel the need to please my kids, my colleagues, my in-laws, my friends? If it's not that clear, ask yourself: What are the things I do in a day or throughout the week for other people? How often do I go with my first choice? Do I play my own music or listen to whatever's being played around me? Take a moment and reflect and then separately consider the following: Where in my life, and with whom, am I trying to control their perception of me?

It's incredible how many of our decisions are made by the tally of everyone else's votes, and yet, is your codependency serving your children? How is it serving your marriage or partnership? How is it serving your career? Your health?

My friend the psychotherapist Terri Cole said that when she started her practice, she noticed a pattern of codependent behaviors in her clients. When she brought it up to them and said, "I think you're suffering from codependency," a majority of her clients reacted with statements like, "What are you, crazy? Everyone's dependent on me, pal. I'm doing everything. I'm the go-to person. I'm the fixer. I'm making all the cash."

"Right. That's still codependency."

Terri calls this high-functioning codependency. These clients saw themselves as martyrs because they would overgive, overfunction, and self-abandon. They put themselves as the last on their own lists for decades. But it wasn't only her clients who did this. She had also been through it herself.

In her late twenties, Terri's sister was in a toxic, abusive relationship with a crack addict, living in the middle of the woods in a house with no running water. Terri tried to help by talking to her sister and sending money, then crying to her therapist and her husband about her sister's problems. She didn't realize it was such a compulsion or that she was choosing to do those things. Most importantly, Terri didn't realize that after every call with her sister, she felt like a toxic dump had just been, well, dumped on her.

One day her therapist said, "Let me ask you something. What makes you think you know what your sister needs to learn in this life, on her life journey?"

"Well, I think we can all agree she doesn't need to learn it in a freaking house in the woods with a crack addict beating her."

"No, I definitely can agree. But do you know what's happening for you? Your sister's dumpster fire of a life is really messing with your peace. So yes, of course you love her, but do you want her life to ruin your peace? It's not your life to fix." Her therapist then pointed out, "You think you're helping, but really, you're probably impeding the process. She's got to reach a certain place in her own life. And you don't have to listen to her talk to you about this abusive relationship she's in. It's not yours to solve, change, or fix."

The therapist suggested that Terri call her sister and say, "Hey, I love you. But talking to you about this idiot that you're living with is too painful. So just know that I'm going to step back. But if and when you're ever actually ready to get out of this horrible situation, I'm still your person."

Terri made the call to her sister. For the next nine months, they only talked a few times. Then one day, her sister said, "I'm ready." Terri got in her car and went to get her. Her sister got sober and eventually became a nurse.

We spend so much energy at the expense of our own well-being trying to hold for everyone else. It's trying to do the impossible. We think this act of becoming Superwoman is going to help, but it's never what's best for the other person. We don't know what's best for their life journey. So please stop taking responsibility for every human being who crosses your path. This is your permission slip to let yourself off the hook.

When you are focused on people-pleasing, you are not being the greatest expression of yourself. The person who aims to please everyone cannot have a point of view and they cannot freely create. The people pleaser shrinks. They wilt. They disappear. And, again, don't mistake disappearing or stepping back as an act of support or generosity. Because it's not. Relationships, in order to be healthy and honest, must be free of codependency, free of feeling responsible for other people's reactions. To be in relationship wholeness, both people must only be responsible for themselves, and both people must feel free to express themselves authentically. Truly loving someone else means respecting their autonomy. Truly loving yourself means staying true to yourself. Staying true to yourself means being that much closer to tuning into abundance.

**You get to be generous.
You get to be supportive.
You get to be *all* those things,
and be true to yourself.**

With all of this in mind, grab a pen and a piece of paper and complete the following prompts:

If I didn't need to be liked, I would say _____

_____

_____

_____

If I didn't need approval, I would go and do _____

_____

_____

_____

If I didn't feel the need to please, I would create _____

_____

_____

_____

How do those answers make you feel? Excited? Empowered? More authentically you? Or do your answers invoke a little fear, some resistance?

As someone who grew up wanting to keep the peace around me and desperately trying to be liked, it has taken me a long time to unravel from this narrative, and I can still get caught up from time to time. I'll do something in an unconscious effort to be more likable and I'll recognize my old codependency, my automatic need to please, and my willingness to contort myself toward that effort. Shaking free of the codependency to please is hard work—some of the hardest—and yet it can be some of your best work. Because your job is to be you, to offer your authenticity to the world.

Unsubscribe from pleasing everyone. You were not designed to be all things to everyone.

Despite what you may fear, showing up as yourself is less likely to clear a room than to attract more people to it. When you're able to say, "This is me. This is my truth; this is it," you draw people in like a DJ calling everyone to the dance floor. Will everyone join your party? Will everyone dance to your beat? No, because everyone is playing to their own music. But don't let that stop *you* from making your grand entrance. Don't let that stop you from putting your shoulders back, stepping forward and playing to your highest note. When you play to your notes, when you turn up the volume of your authentic self, many people will move in your direction.

How many times have you been with a person who helps you, by the very nature of their energy, to feel more connected to flow? Calmer? More creative? It's because each of us imprints an energy on the world, a resonance that is felt by others.

The way that it works energetically is that we are always moving in the direction of more ease, more bliss, more equanimity, a more receptive mode, but it takes time. You will only be able to tune or to resonate or to influence someone who's within seven degrees of where you are energetically. Anyone who's beyond that can't be tuned by you. They can't feed off of it, they can't hear it, it doesn't register, they're too far away—and this is helpful, because you can't affect the whole world, and you don't need to affect the whole world. You just need to affect the people who are an energetic match, who can be influenced by your tuning because they're within seven degrees of your frequency. That's why it's important to be authentic and to not waste your time trying to influence those who are in their resistance. If they're that far from where you are energetically, they can't hear it. People need to build their own foundation and decide when they're ready, and when they are, you'll be there.

GREAT LEADERS

You cannot be responsible for other people. They get to choose the way they perceive. They get to choose how they show up.

If you think about the great tennis coach Rick Macci, how do you think he coached Serena Williams? He's not going to do her work for her. He's going to demand it from her. He's going to say, "Don't give me this. This is BS. Where are you right now?" That's leadership. Leadership isn't, "Oh Serena, I'm going to play your tennis match. I'm going to lace up your shoes. I'm gonna make sure that you sleep. Make sure you eat. Make sure you're not smoking a cigarette. I'm gonna be responsible for you." That is not his job. That's called a babysitter. That's not a leader.

A leader means I see you, period. And a leader means I see a vision that's further than the one you saw, and I'm going to keep pointing you toward it.

That's it. Remember what JFK said: "Ask not what your country can do for you—ask what you can do for your country." You do it.

Why is his magic still in the hearts and souls of anyone who's ever heard him or lived through that? Because he said to everyone, I don't care what you look like. I don't care where you come from. You're needed here and let's go. And people said, Oh my God, he's right. That's what leaders do. Leaders make leaders.

Everyone's a spark of the divine. Everybody has that same capacity. Please don't make yourself responsible for other people, because you'll make them shrink. They're grown adults. They have a creator, and it's not you. Don't try to do God's job.

When we stop seeking or needing others to cosign for us, we not only set ourselves free but also grant permission to others to be their authentic selves. When we free ourselves from being everyone's favorite by detaching from the way others react to us, when we stop trying to control how others perceive us or how they react in the world, *period*, we are expressing true generosity, support, and love toward others and ourselves. The people around us win *big* when we stand firmly in our authenticity because it encourages them to follow suit, to show up fully as themselves and have their own experience.

**Free yourself from being everyone's favorite.
Be yourself and love others enough
to allow them their experience.**

8.

WORTHY OF MORE

RECENTLY I HAD one of those mornings when I felt triggered with a capital T, and I could not get out of it. I stubbornly held on to my horrible mood as if I were trying to prove something. Do you ever have days like this? It started on the drive to a noontime school performance for my youngest daughter. My husband reached across the seats to hold my hand, and I pulled away. I said, "Not right now. I'm in a bad mood; don't even come close to me."

And it got worse.

We arrived at the school and as we walked into the auditorium, I broke off to sit by myself. That's right—I watched the entire performance several rows away from my family, who continued to wave me back to sit with them. I wouldn't budge. Afterward, on the ride home, Lowell quietly asked, "Did you like sitting by yourself?" and I responded curtly, "Yes, I enjoyed being alone." He nodded and continued driving, and as if I hadn't held onto my bad mood long enough, when we returned home, I started in on him—*Why haven't you done this? Why didn't you do that?* Again, Lowell responded calm and cool: "It's okay, I've got it." And then—get this—he made me lunch, and not just any lunch. He made me one of my most favorite things, avocado toast and a fruit smoothie. He set both down next to me, along with a cookie. It was the kindest gesture. And what did I do? I said, "I already ordered lunch. DoorDash will be here any minute."

I told you; I was clutching my bad mood as if my life depended on it.

Lowell said, "All right, we can eat that later. I hope you like your lunch."

He walked out of my office and quietly closed the door. And I started to cry. I was struck by his unwavering kindness. I'd been so horrible to him, and he didn't lower his frequency to match mine. He stayed resolutely parked higher up the radio dial, and this forced me to listen to my own music. Left alone in my office, I tuned into myself and heard a familiar song, a lonely song thick with the theme of abandonment. I unconsciously wrote this song about myself when my father walked out on my family when I was still in middle school. After he left, my grandmother said, "Your father's not only divorcing your mom; he's divorcing his kids too." I didn't hear from my dad for a while after he left, and within that time, my mother spiraled deeper into mental instability. It was an isolating time for me. I often felt as though I didn't exist, as if I didn't matter. And those feelings of separation and lack created a lyric—a limiting belief—that I wasn't worthy, that I wasn't enough. And that lyric has played throughout my life at different volumes and at different times.

In workshops, when I ask women, "Would you love to have more joy? Would you love to take better care of yourself? Would you like a beautiful home? Would you love to travel with your kids to Greece?" the answer I get nine times out of ten is—

Yes, but . . .

Yes, but I don't need it.

Yes, but I don't want to appear greedy.

Yes, but I don't want to seem materialistic.

Yes, but I don't deserve it.

Yes, but I won't get it.

Yes, but it'll never happen, so why wish for it?

There is a deep reckoning that far too many of us must do around our unworthiness. If you are living with less than you want and deserve, it's because you've created resistance. There is static in your reception. A disruption in the flow. We're each meant to have clear access to the infinite stream of abundance that is available to *everyone*, and tapping into abundance doesn't make you greedy or gross or entitled or corrupt. There is no judgment. There is nothing you have to justify. Receiving abundance is just a choice to be a bigger vessel. Every one of us living on the planet is meant to receive, and as we do, we are giving to the whole ecosystem.

Here's a metaphor I like to share to get the idea across. My family is Jewish but I love Christmas. I love Christmas lights, Christmas music, all the festivities. During the pandemic I wanted the holidays to feel totally over the moon, so I hired some guys to bring a ridiculous amount of Christmas lights to my house. It was like Chevy Chase in *National Lampoon's Christmas Vacation*. We had a blow-up version of Buddy the Elf and Rudolph in the front yard, plus lights on every tree, lights throughout every room, upstairs and down.

My husband kept saying, "This is not going to happen. It's not going to work."

I thought, *What does he know?*

Turns out, he was right. The lights kept blowing out; the refrigerator turned off. Rudolph was deflated on the lawn and Will Ferrell in Buddy the Elf form was all scrunched up. I finally had to ask the electrician what was going on. He told me, "You don't have enough wattage here in the electric panel to hold all this charge. You'd have to add to the breaker to hold more."

Well, we didn't add a breaker, and my Christmas vision didn't turn out the way I'd hoped, but on the bright side it gave me a great analogy for manifesting. If you want to allow more into your life, you must have the capacity to energetically hold more. Think about your life right now: How comfortable or uncomfortable are you receiving a compliment or when a friend offers to pay for dinner? When we are identified with our ego, we can only receive so much energy. But if we feel connected to our soul, when we feel one with Source, then we can receive an infinite amount of energy because it flows through us like an infinite loop.

YOU GET WHAT you have the courage to ask for. And you get what you have the capacity to receive. So often I meet women and ask them, "Where in your life do you feel reciprocity? Where do you feel real energetic exchange in your life? Where have you created that, because you will be amazed at how people will show up the way you teach them to show up for you." If in our lives we are carrying a thimble-size capacity to receive and we overgive at the same time, we're depleted and we don't have the capacity to receive. We don't have to gaslight ourselves; we can feel the sense of worthiness that allows us to be available for a much higher standard of care, and that starts by putting that yummy lotion on your hands. It starts by taking a bath, and not a rushed, ordinary kind of bath—you take beautiful flowers and rose quartz and you put them in the bath and you take twenty-five minutes to soak in it. It's so important to retrain yourself, to re-teach yourself what to expect from life. This is the energetic signature you send out. It starts to be felt in the field, and that is how the world perceives and responds to you.

TAKE A BATH

Here's what I would love for you to do. Take a bath. You might think, *Whoa, this is kind of rebellious and impractical when I have fifty other things to do right now*, but I think it'll be powerful.

As you fill up the bathtub, set the intention that you're going to soak into that divine feminine-aligned, potent, conscious, beautiful energy. Set the intention to release your unconscious addiction to the struggle, and come back to your body in the present moment. Set the intention that while you're in the bath, you're going to allow this beautiful, incredible gift called "life" to soften and soak into you.

I would suggest that if you can, put on a spa playlist that can play in the background to create the environment. Then place your phone away from you so you can't touch it.

I'm curious what that feels like. Because for us to have an impact on the rest of our day and tomorrow and our life, we need a different energetic imprint, and we need to come from more ease in our nervous system. We don't have so much familiarity with fully nourishing ourselves and filling our cups. I know that it can seem like such an unproductive, silly thing to do in the middle of the day, but it actually is one of the most meaningful gestures that you can make for yourself.

Now, if for some reason you don't have access to a bath or that is something that is so far out of your comfort zone that you just don't want to do it, then do something similar. Put your phone away and for ten minutes allow yourself to just soak into this divine, connected, aligned place within yourself. Just allow the moment to wrap you up. This is well worth ten to fifteen minutes of your time.

I highly recommend taking a moment to really stop and let yourself soak in this energy. As crazy as it seems, since we've been taught to put all our attention elsewhere, this work is really the doorway to the portal, because you are learning in real time how to create a sanctuary within yourself—and that sanctuary within you unlocks the door to further expansion.

When we make a habit of embodying and coming home to and tending to the place within us, the deep sanctuary space that is beyond the mind, that is gentle, that is soft, that is connected to the divine, we find tremendous wisdom, wholeness, and abundance. Time slows down, and we wind up being present for our life. We wind up being directed by the wisdom within us.

Here are some affirmations that can be helpful to repeat daily or whenever you feel the need to connect with the sanctuary within yourself. Allow them to resonate within you and guide you toward a state of receptivity, peace, and alignment with your true self.

- I am open and receptive to the gentle flow of divine energy.
- I trust in the unfolding of divine timing and surrender to its wisdom.
- I allow myself to receive and embrace the nurturing energy of the universe.

- I am a vessel of love and compassion, radiating peace and tranquility.
- I honor and respect my intuition, following its guidance with grace and ease.
- I release the need for control, allowing the universe to support me effortlessly.
- I am worthy of receiving abundance and blessings in all areas of my life.
- I embrace my feminine essence and celebrate the power of softness and vulnerability.
- I am connected to the wisdom and strength of my divine feminine energy.
- I surrender to the natural rhythms of life, finding harmony in rest and rejuvenation.
- I trust in the divine plan for my life and have faith in its perfect unfolding.
- I release any resistance and welcome the abundant blessings that flow to me.
- I am a magnet for love, joy, and all the blessings of the universe.
- I honor my emotions and allow myself to feel deeply and authentically.
- I am in tune with the cycles of nature and embrace the beauty of divine timing.

Once you've cycled through the affirmations, shift your perspective backward and remember yourself as a little child. Can you picture yourself at seven years old? Do you have an image that comes to mind? Were you missing a tooth? Did you have this pair of red sneakers that you loved? Picture that kid and notice how effortless it is to see the goodness in the younger version of yourself. Do you see it? Do you see your innocent self? She was *there*, and at some point along the way, your mind created an unconscious story. And that story communicated to you in some way, shape, or form one of two lies: either that you're not enough or that it's not possible. Neither is true. You're more than enough, and it is completely possible.

I had Dr. Jennifer Wallace on my podcast and we were talking about her book, *Never Enough: When Achievement Culture Becomes Toxic*. She did a ton of research and found out something fascinating that points to women and our relationship with self-care. She said, "The number one intervention for any child in distress is to make sure the primary caregivers, most often the mothers, prioritize their well-being, their mental health and make sure their support system is intact because a child's resilience rests fundamentally on the resilience of their mother. And a mother's resilience rests fundamentally on her relationships, the depth and support of those relationships."

Jennifer said, "We are sold a bill of goods by the wellness industry that if we light a candle and drink tea, we will be resilient. Those are certainly great and can be stress reducers, but they will not give you the resilience you need to be, as researchers call us, the first responders to our kids' struggles.

"We need people in our lives, one or two or three friends who we can be vulnerable with, who we can open up to, who we feel unconditionally loved and supported, just like the people we try to be for our own kids. We need to invest in our relationships outside of the home for our children's benefit. It is not just about putting your oxygen mask on first. It is about having one or two or three friends in your life who know you intimately, who can see you gasping for air and who reach and put that oxygen mask on for you. That's a whole other level of friendship."

So, why is it so hard to open up to more? What creates the resistance?

Old stories, old lyrics, another spin around the turntable.

When I talked with clinical psychologist Dr. Shefali, she said that the core for the evolution and healing of the world is the consciousness of the mother figure. As she dug deeper into her research, she realized that the biggest curse on the planet is women not being receivers. When a mother figure is so attached to her ego and her false identity, it gets passed down. As I like to say, "It's not what's taught. It's what's caught." The next generation doesn't get a chance at their own destiny. If we were raised by mothers who were stuck in ego, who did not believe that they were worthy of abundance, it's likely that their limiting beliefs about receiving were imprinted on us. And if we continue that unconscious pattern, we teach our sons and daughters not to receive as well.

I was coaching a woman in my online membership community who was struggling with a common receptivity issue. She felt scared of stepping into her power, being unapologetically herself. She wasn't aware of how much she was wanting to be liked and trying to be sweet because she had always played that role in her family growing up. I walked her through a practice that helped her, which you can also try.

Read through this exercise and then give it a try.

Close your eyes.

Scan your life through your teen years, your twenties, your thirties, and your forties, looking for evidence around the belief that "I am safe as long as I'm not fully in my power. It is not safe to be powerful." Take some time to go back. See if any experiences or pieces of evidence come up. How do they show up? Feel into this unconscious belief that takes up a lot of space.

As you remember and experience a moment when you believed that, feel yourself now as the powerful, wise woman you are, clearing the belief because you know what's actually true.

Move it. Clear it.

Tell that younger you: "You're safe to be authentic. You're safe to be powerful. The world can handle it."

When you're ready, open your eyes.

FOR WHAT IT'S WORTH

You are either receptive, allowing abundance into your life, or you are resistant. You're coming from either a place of "yes" or a place of "no." It's that simple; it's that black-and-white. Which is it for you? When you feel into your energy, in which direction is it pulled? Receiving is inherent and resistance is learned, so if your life isn't flowing easily—if you're in debt, there's no money, no thriving, only stagnation, or if there are certain things that you've wanted for a very long time and they haven't shown up—it is likely due to a learned belief or behavior that you're unconsciously attuned to. And if you're a woman, the line backward tends to point in the direction of the matriarch in your family, so take a few minutes now and answer these questions about your grandmother, then repeat them for your mother, and then answer them a third time for yourself.

What was your grandmother's/mother's sense of worthiness? What is my sense of worthiness?

_____

_____

_____

_____

_____

_____

How worthy did your grandmother/mother feel? How worthy do I feel?

_____

_____

_____

_____

_____

_____

_____

How did your grandmother/mother receive in her life? How do I receive in my life?

_____

_____

_____

_____

What was your grandmother's/mother's relationship with money? What is my relationship with money?

_____

_____

_____

_____

Did your grandmother/mother feel empowered to earn? To accept and accumulate wealth? Do I feel empowered to earn? To accept and accumulate wealth?

_____

_____

_____

_____

Finally, how did your grandmother/mother define wealth and abundance? How do I define wealth and abundance?

_____

_____

_____

_____

MONEY, NOT CREATED IN A VACUUM

When I ask attendees in my workshops to contemplate their learned and often unconscious beliefs about money, they instantly recall hearing statements like these:

You have to be a snob to have money.

Money is hard to come by.

People with money are righteous jerks.

Money is hard to make.

Money is a pain.

People with money are evil.

Money is hard earned.

Money does not equal happiness.

Money doesn't grow on trees.

Money's not available.

There is always a lot of judgment about money. And do you notice how these statements start to sound starkly similar? They all carry a similar vibration of scarcity and lack, of separation and unworthiness. Now, consider the effect that these unconscious beliefs have on the person lugging them around. If you think money is a disgusting thing, corrupt and greedy or something reserved for only a select few (excluding you), then why would you allow it into your life? If money is the root of pain, rejection, isolation, or disruption, of course you unconsciously resist it. When you start to understand your perception of money in the context of limiting beliefs and in the context of stories passed down to you, the numbers in your bank account begin to make a whole lot more sense.

My grandmother Betty was from the Ukraine. Around 1918 her family settled in America in a tenement on the Lower East Side of Manhattan. In the building where she lived with her parents and siblings, there was only one toilet to serve twenty-six families, and as a result, many people got sick and died of tuberculosis. In those days, girls were not allowed to go to school past fifth grade; so, at a young age my grandmother was working in a sweatshop and cutting hair. At the end of every week, she'd give her earnings to her father, who would greedily take the money from her and spend it on her brothers, leaving her with nothing. She had no money, to the point where she would take an eyeliner pencil and draw a line up the back of her leg to look like she had pantyhose on because she couldn't afford stockings.

Even through all of this, she had the courage to dance through life. I mean that both literally and figuratively, because she was a very talented dancer. She used to always find that higher vibration, and she danced her way through everything. (By the way, fun fact—my grandmother danced at a really famous club in New York City called the Roseland Ballroom, where Ella Fitzgerald regularly sang.) My grandmother had barely a penny to her name, and considering all the circumstances she grew up with, she had every good reason to cry. Instead, she chose to dance. She chose to enjoy what she had in the moment. That was one of the most beautiful life lessons she taught me.

Like most people we know, my grandmother was also a complex mosaic of things. Once she married my grandfather, she was lifted incrementally out of poverty. But when she became a widow at sixty, she had never written a check, never paid for anything on her own. She felt financially insecure and passed this insecurity down to my mother, who never felt empowered with money. In the 1970s, my mom earned her own money as an elementary school teacher, but every penny she made went to pay back her parents for money they had lent my parents to buy a house. When she became a mother, she left her teaching job at the elementary school. She then became a piano teacher and taught lessons at home in the afternoons. My dad was resentful that she didn't make more money, and she felt like whatever she did—take care of my sister and me, clean the house, and so on—was never enough. My father underscored this message, even if he didn't say it, by intimating that because Mom wasn't working a full-time job, she wasn't an equal partner in the marriage. Eventually, Dad left, and after he remarried, he praised his new wife for being a career woman. I unconsciously learned from my father that to be a good spouse, a woman needed to contribute at least equally to be considered a good partner. I also learned that if a woman didn't have her own money, her spouse could leave and she would wind up with nothing. It's no wonder that I felt so driven to become the provider in my own marriage years later. It created a lot of pain in my dynamic with my husband. Even now that I'm aware of it, I can still fall back into a pattern of insecurity and doubt.

Gay Hendricks, psychologist and author of *The Big Leap*, proposes that we all have an unconscious set point based on what we believe and that we cannot push past that set point until we fundamentally change our beliefs. To have more abundance in your life, it is imperative to remove sticky static from the line, and the first step to doing this requires an awareness that any limited views you have about money likely belong to other people. Said another way, the song you're singing about money is one you picked up when you weren't paying attention, and over the course of your life, it's become an earworm that you can't shake and that you've claimed as your own. If you've been tuned to the key of limitation, to the string of "money doesn't grow on trees" because that's the music that was played in your home growing up, then guess what? You have unconsciously resonated with that belief. You're vibrating at the frequency of scarcity, where the world appears desolate and scary. It's the soundtrack to every dystopian film, and you're playing it. Yeah, that's a bummer, but it's okay. That's awareness. And awareness creates a path forward, a new song to sing. When you tune yourself to the higher notes of "I am worthy of financial abundance" and "There is no shame in receiving," you'll begin to resonate at a higher frequency—and from there, the numbers will change.

As I'll continue to share, it took me nearly my entire lifetime to unravel from the "good girl" and the "good wife" narrative and to change my old belief that money will corrupt me and make me unrelatable to real people, including my own children, my husband, and maybe also my cats. Like they say, it's been a journey, and often an uncomfortable one, but unraveling myself from old lyrics is valuable work. So many of us carry whisperings from our past, from the women who came before us, who were told to "be good." To follow the rules. To stand in line. To not ask for more because they *didn't deserve more*. The way to break free is to recognize the unconscious narrative and generational patterns about abundance that are not consistent with allowing it into your experience.

Speaking of which, I had an experience that really shined a light on some of my issues with receiving. When Lowell and I were engaged, I needed a new car. My lease was up, and he went car shopping with me. We figured it was smart to get a bigger car than I had in case we had a baby within the next few years. After test-driving a few SUVs, we chose the Acura RDX, which was zippy enough while still feeling roomy for a new family. The night we went to get the car, Lowell told me he would talk to the dealership manager alone to try to help me get the best deal before I went in and signed the paperwork. Remember, we weren't married yet and I needed a new car. Later that evening Lowell walked over to me with the keys to my new car and said, "Congrats, I bought it for you." I couldn't believe it. I started to cry and begged him to take it back so I could pay for it myself. I was beside myself. I felt so overwhelmed with a sense of unworthiness and obligation. Lowell explained that he felt it was a responsible decision since we were going to be married in three months. My reaction was so crazy that it taught me a lot about my sense of feeling worthy. We went to see a therapist and she told me that Lowell would buy me the world if he knew it would make me happy. She told me that one of the most loving things I could ever do was to let someone feel needed and to receive from them. This was and still is a major paradigm shift in my life. The Hebrew word for love is *Ahava*. The root of the word is *Hav*. *Hav* means to give. Love is actually about giving. One of the most beautiful ways we give to someone is to let them feel needed and to receive the love they want to give us. I am still working on this and softening my guard to allowing for that love and intimacy to flow into my heart.

NOTICE WHAT YOU allow yourself to receive. Allowance is the key word here, and it can be very simple: receiving a compliment, a gift, an offer of assistance, an open door. A moment like this came up for me recently with a friend, except I was the giver and she was the receiver. We were out to dinner and when the server brought us the check, she said to my friend and me, "Do you want me to split it down the middle?" I jumped in, "No, I'll pay for it." My friend smiled and graciously accepted my offer to pay, but I sensed some discomfort, some hesitation on her part, and this was interesting to me. I wondered to myself, *Why is this making her uncomfortable?* What is it about receiving that makes *any of us* uncomfortable? Is it obligation? In the case of my friend, did she think that if she accepted my gesture today, she'd be on the hook to pay for our next dinner out? Was it guilt? *If I let Cathy pay, then that means I'm coasting for free.* Or does our discomfort with receiving go deeper than that—

I don't feel like I deserve it.
I am a burden.
I am not worthy.

This dynamic comes through in other kinds of relationships too. I was coaching a woman whose husband used to live in scarcity, so she dimmed her light to play to his level. She looked to buy things on sale because she thought, *Well, he thinks it's better to spend less, so I should find the better deal.* But then he got a new career that bumped up his income and introduced him to an abundant way of living and thinking, and she felt like she was still stuck with that scarcity mentality.

I told her, "Dimming down is no longer necessary, if it ever was. Let yourself shine! That presence is a gift to your relationship."

In fact, the Talmud says that a woman brings mazel to a man and that every child doubles that mazel. It also says that if a man without integrity marries a righteous woman, he'll become righteous. And if a righteous man marries a woman without integrity, he'll become evil. That's how powerful the connection is within our partnerships.

We can't get stuck in the separation illusion of "Well, if he's created this, then who am I to play with the spoils?" You've co-created it. And the more you receive, the more your partner is going to make, and the more that you're going to keep bumping into abundance together, and who knows—you might be the muse, and he might bring opportunities that match your vibration, and vice versa. Together you're creating this power-ful atom bomb, this nucleus. It's a love-splosion.

Your biggest gift to your relationship is to be a receiver. If a man feels that his wife is available to receive, he'll literally go build her the world. Men love to give. They love it. They feel such an ego boost if they can give you an orgasm, if they can give you pleasure, if they can give you the tool to open that bottle with the pesky cap. Giving love in any way doubles and triples their capacity to generate more. So, allow it!

If you are someone who pushes away the gifts that the world and people offer you, check your limiting beliefs. Question them and update your story: I *have* thoughts. I am not my thoughts. I am not the old story. I am not the lyric about limitation and lack. I am worthy to receive. Say it—

I am worthy to receive abundance.

Say it again.

You are worthy because a soul is worthy. It doesn't have to earn its worth.

You are a soul that is connected to the abundant energy of the universe, the *highest* frequency on the radio dial. When you allow yourself to make space for what's flowing in your direction without turning away from or blocking that channel, you align with the abundant energy of the universe that is continuously moving toward balance, peace, and wholeness. Toward endless possibility.

NOW, CATHY, you ask, *if my patterns are "unconscious," how will I know that I'm replicating them?*

Good catch, and great question! When we hold unconscious beliefs, we're typically also holding shame. Shame for not being enough, for not feeling worthy, for not feeling deserving. So, then, your first clue that you're replicating unconscious beliefs in your own life is feeling shame.

The next thing to check in with is your level of exhaustion. When you push your worthiness down and close off your ability to receive, it's like holding a balloon under water. It takes tremendous effort and resistance to hold a balloon underwater. Have you ever tried doing this? Well, I have and it's a tiresome endeavor, and if you're similarly holding yourself down and apart from receiving, you might also feel like you're going to imminently *pop*! Moving forward, check in with your level of shame, especially around the subject of money. Listen to your thoughts. What are they saying? Are they singing a tune of limitation or abundance? Of worthlessness or worthiness?

PAUSE THE SONG

The unconscious lyrics of limitation project a world before us that looks desolate, scarce, and scary. And while we cannot stop ourselves from thinking, we can choose our response. When you're spinning an old story, an old lyric, or a limiting belief from the past that makes you feel ashamed, undeserving, and not enough, the most effective way I know of to pause the song and to change the dial is through the breath. My friend and colleague Samantha Skelly describes the breath as our "life force." If the nature of our life force is abundance, she argues, our breath is the connecting force. She says, "When we breathe deeply and intentionally, we can remove the stagnation, the stories about scarcity and the static from our lives."

This next exercise combines breath work with affirmations to shift your energy from resistance to receiving. Get comfortable in your chair and take several deep breaths in and out. As you continue to breathe, can you connect with the part of yourself that is bigger than your story, that goes beyond your mind? Can you connect with the part of yourself that is separate from your past, from the people who came before you? Can you connect with the part of yourself that is present in this moment? Once you relax into your body, repeat after me:

I am worthy, exactly as I am.
What would it feel like to release the need for external validation,
and embrace my inherent worthiness?
I am deserving of all the good that life has to offer.
What if I was worthy to pursue all that I desire?
I am a master manifester. My thoughts turn to things.
I am aligning with the energy of receiving.
I am open to becoming wealthy.
I am worthy of financial abundance.
There is no shame in receiving.
I am surrendering financial worry.
I am releasing scarcity thinking.

What if money was a tool to create positive change in the world?
I am in the process of trusting that the universe is guiding me toward abundance.
What if abundance is mine because *I am* abundant? I am unlimited.

Make a habit of revisiting these thoughts every day. Add them to your morning meditation, that most important daily meeting with yourself. This is how you change the dial: by singing a *new* tune, over and over again. When you start humming a different lyric that speaks of greater self-worth and abundance, you begin to rewire the neural pathways in your mind, and this expands the restrictions of the small self—the good girl who learned to please others by diminishing her needs and dimming down—by giving her a stronger voice and stretching her capacity to receive.

I AM

When I had Deepak Chopra on my podcast, he told me that our ultimate purpose in life is to know who we are. He said, "Nobody knows who they are. Are you your body? Well, which one? The fertilized egg? Zygote? Which one? You don't have a body. It's an activity, a perceptual activity. Some people will say I'm my mind. Which one? You had a different mind when you were a teenager. Others say, I'm my personality. Well, hopefully that is evolving." What Deepak was getting at is that who you are is really the infinite, the divine pretending to be a person. It's the most joyous thing that can be experienced.

Our relationship to who we are and to self is so crucial because it also impacts our worthiness. Deepak pointed out that the number two cause of death of people under eighteen years old in this country is suicide. What does that tell you? It tells you that people don't understand what real worthiness is. They don't understand the most essential thing, which is that we are all inherently worthy. That's who we are. I am worthy.

He said to me, "Say, 'I am Cathy Heller.' Say it three times."

I said it: "I am Cathy Heller. I am Cathy Heller. I am Cathy Heller."

"How does it feel?"

"Okay, I guess."

"Great. Now just say, 'I'm Cathy.'"

"I'm Cathy."

"Does that feel different? Now just say, 'I am.'"

"I am."

The point of this exercise was to show how the I Am is so much bigger than our name, bigger than our body. You are part of this Oneness. You are the I Am. That's the consciousness that runs through you. What is the worthiness of that? Well, it's the totality of all things, everywhere all at once.

This reminds me of something that Rabbi Aaron and I discussed. He said, "Animals do what they feel like doing. Human beings can do what they don't feel like doing. Humans can say, I feel like being mean, or I choose to be kind. I feel like screaming at my kids, or I choose to hold back and smile and compliment them. I choose not to get angry. This is when you embody divinity, when you choose good, when you make the courageous choice to be yourself, your godly, inherently worthy self."

You can have it all if you're willing to let go of the belief that you cannot have it.

At times, when I question my worthiness, I empower the breath. I inhale to the count of four, hold my breath to the count of four, and exhale to the count of eight. I repeat this meditative breathing sequence a few times, and on the last exhale, my head will begin to clear and my vision will expand. It's in the stillness, to which our ear delightfully attunes. It's within that space where we meet our true self, our infinite, abundant self who has all the right answers. In the pause between my own notes, I hear, *I am worthy, exactly as I am, and I am deserving of all the good that life has to offer.*

9.

THE WEALTHY WOMAN WITHIN

VIVIDLY REMEMBER my first-year performance and salary review when I was working at the commercial real estate office. I was one of five agents, and the only woman, and I remember sitting down across from the CEO. He said to me, "Cathy, you've done really well. You made $75,000 in commissions alone. You've had a great year. Are you satisfied with that? Or do you want to make more money? And if so, how much do you think you deserve?"

I shifted backward in my chair, suddenly uncomfortable. Was this a trick question? In my head, I was screaming, *Hell, yeah, I want to make more money!* But, face-to-face with the big boss, I was nervous to ask for it. As he waited for an answer, I finally blurted, "I want to make $100,000 base salary, plus my commission."

I knew this was a significant jump, a sizable ask, and as soon as I asked for it, I half-expected him to laugh or flat-out say no—but he surprised me. He agreed without hesitation. "Done." He smiled. "And again, great work."

I walked out of his office feeling like I'd won the jackpot.

As I returned to my desk, I passed Ryan, another agent, who winked. "My turn."

I knew that, comparatively, I was closing far more deals than Ryan. I mean, the CEO took me out on the golf course with him to woo clients and close deals, and he went so far as to call me his "Wing Woman," so naturally, I wondered what Ryan would ask for and what he'd receive. When he walked past my desk twenty minutes later, I leaned over and whispered, "Hey, how'd your meeting go?"

"Outstanding." He smiled smugly.

"Did you get what you asked for?" I returned the smile and added, "I did."

"Oh, yeah? What did you ask for?"

"One hundred thousand," I said proudly. "What about you?"

"He gave me $150,000 base salary and double the commission."

"What?!" I raised my voice. Did I hear him wrong? "One hundred and fifty thousand?"

"Yep."

"But, how?" I protested. "I've been here longer than you. I've done more deals than you. Why did you get that much?"

Ryan shrugged. "He asked me, 'What do you feel like you deserve?' And I told him I deserved $150,000 base salary and double the commission."

I was shocked, and pissed, to be honest. I stood up and marched down the hall to my boss's office. I walked in without knocking and said, "Hey, I just talked to Ryan, and I want the same salary bump as him."

"Not gonna happen," my boss replied.

"Why?"

"Because I gave you what you told me you deserved, and I gave him what he told me he deserved. And that's that."

Boom. And that was that.

This was such an impactful moment for me. In an instant, it taught me so much about how I valued myself and what I believed I deserved. More importantly, it clarified how closely my self-worth was tied to my net worth, and how the world directly responds to what we think we're worth.

You can have it all once you're willing to let go of the belief that you aren't worthy.

Worthiness grows from within, and it is sparked by granting ourselves freedom from external pleasing. It thrives from believing in oneself. When you tap into your inherent value and worth, you begin to feel more alive, more sexy, more energetic, *more abundant*!

In the early days of my podcast, I'd fantasize about all the abundant women I wanted to have on the show: Brené Brown, Carole King, and Reese Witherspoon. To me, these women exemplify abundance, and not because of their vast influence, earning potential, and fierce styling but because of their unapologetic *presence in the world*. Not unlike how I described His Holiness the Dalai Lama earlier—these women exude a lightness in their own being. Their energy radiates outward and it energizes the room, whether it's the world of fashion, the silver screen, or Carnegie Hall. And this type of magnetism isn't reserved only for celebrities. We each know women like this in our own lives. Women who have presence, who have palpable, positive energy and self-worth. We feel it when they walk into a room. Every smile, every move, every toss of their hair is electrifying. They turn heads, stop people in their tracks, and inevitably draw in crowds around them. Women who walk into a room with a clear and strong energy get served first at a crowded bar and moved to the front of the line. And let's be truthful about this— being the woman who *doesn't* get served first, or served at all, really stinks. Am I right? It's natural to feel envious of women who appear to easily attract love and friendships, money and resources, and amazing opportunities into their lives. I had a college roommate like this—she was a look-alike for Anne Hathaway with a great boyfriend, a beautiful body, and top grades, and she always had available credit on her meal card and friends to hang out with at parties. I'd catch myself thinking, *Why does she get to have all that?* Envy can easily arise in the face of others' good fortune, yet we ought to recognize these people for who they are—all these souls who are enjoying beautiful abundance are clearing a path for *you.* They are serving as examples, showing you what's possible in your own life.

When I had actress Priyanka Chopra on the podcast, she said, "Women have been taught that to be the most popular one in the school, you have to step on the shoulders of everyone else. No. We are going to be so successful as a community, as a world, if we support our women, and if women give each other encouragement. So next time you see another girl trying to do her best, at her job or at her life, just appreciate her. That's all it takes. Just appreciate her and say, you did so great today, you look amazing today. That dress is freaking awesome. It makes such a difference to create a sense of positivity, instead of the negativity that we've been taught that we should have against each other."

We have been taught to be envious, to believe that if one woman *has* that means another woman *has not.* We have been taught that good things are scarce. We need to relearn our perception of the world, because the truth is this: we live in abundance. The more others have, the more we can have. We need to learn to love success in others. When we see someone who has it all, we need to praise her, wish her well, and thank her for lighting a path.

Don't be envious. Thank them for lighting a path and follow their lead.

Women have been taught that there are so few opportunities for us that in order to succeed we have to tear each other down and elbow out the next girl, because if she has more, we have less. This is a common mathematical misconception, and if it's one you've also bought into, let me ask you this: Does everyone deserve to feel healthy? Yes, right? And if you and I are feeling healthy and good, it doesn't rob someone else of feeling healthy and good, right? There's enough health to go around. Okay, next. Does everyone deserve to feel love? Again, yes, right? We all deserve to find, feel, and give and receive love. And if you find love, it doesn't rob someone else of feeling love, right? Because there's an infinite amount of love. It doesn't run out. It's endless.

Final question: Does everyone deserve to be wealthy? To receive abundance?

If you're hesitating to answer, it's likely because you've bought into the false idea that money is a limited resource. This is old programming, an outdated song, and it no longer serves you to listen to it. Abundance is an endless frequency available to everyone. It's a birthright available to everyone, like love and health and happiness. Abundance is infinite. We are each meant to thrive. Everything in nature is designed to live to its potential. So, when you see a woman having the courage to put herself out there, praise her! And when she is successful, celebrate her! It's time to link arms and reject the culture of criticism that says "Who does she think she is?" and replace it with respect—"Thank you for paving the way for me." And while you're thanking her, trust in your own abundance. It's there. It's hidden in plain sight. You can be that woman who walks into a room and turns heads. You can have love and friendships, money and resources, and amazing opportunities—just as everyone else. You can have it all once you stop holding yourself back, separate and apart from everyone else. You can have it once you stop thinking and playing small and believing that by becoming powerful you are a threat.

You are a gift. You are not a threat. And the world wants your energy, your presence.

A PROMOTION FROM WITHIN

My friend Sheri Salata, the former copresident of Harpo Studios and OWN, is a perfect example of how women can pave the way. Before she joined the Oprah orbit, Sheri worked in advertising, and when her agency downsized, she was let go. Sheri applied for jobs everywhere, but the market was flooded with applicants, and after many months of searching and not being hired, she decided to get a job at 7-Eleven, where she sold coffee and lottery tickets. True story. She worked tirelessly as a manager at 7-Eleven while staying committed to a bigger dream. Sure enough, one day, she got a call from a woman at *The Oprah Winfrey Show*, who said, "We were looking through a closet and found your résumé, which you must have sent in a while back. If you're still available, we need some extra freelance help doing promo work. It looks like you have a background in advertising. Can you come in for a temp position that lasts a few weeks?"

Uh, yeah.

Sheri promptly quit her job at 7-Eleven and showed up at Harpo Studios, where she worked for three weeks. At the end of the three weeks, they asked her, "Can you stay longer?" She stayed on for another few weeks that turned into more weeks that stretched into months and that became a full-time job and a promotion, followed by another promotion after that. Fast-forward a few short years. One afternoon Sheri was sitting in Oprah Winfrey's dressing room, and Oprah said, "I have chosen the new executive producer that I'm going to announce to the team later today." She'd written the name on a folded piece of paper that she slid over to Sheri, who unfolded the note: it was her.

Sheri went from managing a 7-Eleven to becoming the executive producer of the biggest television show in history. And then she helped start OWN and became the president of Harpo. It's an incredible story, and you're likely wondering, *How did she do it?*

She manifested it. She was appreciative and high vibe, even during her days at 7-Eleven. When she got to the *Oprah Winfrey Show*, she brought her loving energy with her. The most impressive thing is always love. The most powerful person in the room is always the most loving. It didn't matter that she had come from 7-Eleven. What mattered to Oprah was Sheri's energy.

I've coached thousands of women who are so married to an old story of their identity. Most of them have done all the "right things" to try to be the best version of themselves. But still, there's this pandemic of not feeling like they're enough. They don't believe they are worthy, and they don't understand how overqualified they are to love other people and to be present, and that these are always the most important things about a person. When you think of someone who impresses you, it's not the people with the most PhDs or a garage full of Ferraris. It's really the people who truly resonate love. Being impressive has everything to do with how much space you create for love within yourself and for someone else. We live in a time when there is such an empathy deficit. But you are equipped with the greatest gift that the world actually needs and actually finds impressive, which is that you are connected to the love that comes to and through you. That is your superpower. My friend Rabbi Daniel Cohen said that it's not even about trying to change the whole world. Instead, it's about trying to change the world of one person every day—because that will change that one person's whole world. That act is something each one of us can do.

He said, "Mark Twain said the two most important days of your life are the day when you're born and the day when you understand why. And when you're in a particular place, to be that messenger to help somebody again, feel a sense of hope and life and light, you're going to make a huge difference in the world."

He was leading an event a couple years ago about filling the world with acts of kindness, and he asked people to share their stories. One woman said, "I am a NODA nurse at Stanford Hospital. NODA is no one dies alone.

I'm always with patients at the end of their life, just to be there with them. Near the end of this patient's life, I was feeding this patient ice cream. And I felt closer to this patient than ever before." The patient soon passed away. A couple of days later, she learned a remarkable thing about her patient: the patient's father was the doctor who brought her into the world fifty years earlier! And now, the nurse realized, *God has put me in this place to help his child leave the world.* And that's the way we have to see the power of that light, because it will reverberate and it will be eternal.

This is why whenever a woman tells me "I don't think I'm good enough or have enough certifications to help these people," it drives me crazy. Women become resistant to reclaiming their bright and brilliant selves, because their wounded egos are plagued by a fear of being rejected. A fear of being criticized. A fear of failing. A fear of succeeding. A fear of changing. A fear of telling a new story, dancing to a new beat.

Do you know someone like this?

Is it you?

For a long time it was me. And it's time for both of us to lay that down.

It's time to stop thinking we need to be some perfect person that we think the world wants and choose to be authentic.

It's time to stop worrying about pleasing others and to find favor with yourself.

It's time to believe in your own value.

When you begin walking into a room and emanating the energy of self-worth, your inherent value and authenticity, heads will turn and doors will open, my friend. Your very being will beam that same love and acceptance to others, and they'll be magnetized and drawn to you.

SUNSHINE

Grab a pen and paper and draw a big sun. There's a circle in the middle, and then all these lines coming out of it like a sun with beams of light. And in the middle, I want you to write something that you so desire, something that you've been wanting, something that you've been hoping to manifest.

For me, I would write down *home* because, boy, do I have a journey with that, and one day I may write a whole book on that topic. What do you want to write down? A vacation to Italy? A better marriage?

Now I want you to write a word for each of the lines you drew, lines coming out from the circle. I want you to write a feeling that you would experience once you had manifested this wish. What does this dream represent in the feeling sense? What is it going to feel like when you have the million dollars? What is it going to feel like when you have that new home? What is it going to feel like when your dream shows up at your door? How will that feel? Write it down.

In my journal I wrote *home* in the center of the circle, then on the lines I wrote *cozy, peaceful, grounded, love, nourishing equanimity, abundance,* and *stability.* What I know to be true is that the more I look at this, the more I know exactly what the recipe is to manifest the dream. It's to feel all these feelings. And guess what? I don't have to wait to feel what love feels like. I don't have to wait to feel what coziness feels like to me in my gut. I don't have to wait to experience what it feels like to be nourished. What starts to happen is as I sit in those feelings, I have thoughts that lead me to an action that matches that outcome. "You know what would feel like being grounded today? Eat this. And do you know what it would feel like to be nourished today? Sit here, look at this, do this." And *because we don't get what we want but we get what we are,* the more our radio is the station that receives these feelings because it knows them and feels them. The more we start to hear that music, which means we see it everywhere. We experience it everywhere. Because it's a mirror, it's always an echo to what's coming from within. And it helps, the more that you get clear about what this feels like. It also helps you understand what you really want. And then you start to perceive new thoughts. And you start realizing that other things you thought were urgent feel a lot less urgent right now. Because that urgency was coming from a creation of the wounded self rather than the wise woman that you are.

FEEL LIGHT IN THE FUTURE

Think back to a time when you felt ease in your life, when you were in flow. Maybe you were the woman at the bar turning heads and being waved to the front of the line. Maybe it was a time when you were working on a project and everything was lining up just right. Maybe you've had a moment when connections and synchronicities were unfolding without effort, and you thought to yourself, *Dang, I am making magic happen!* Think back to a moment when you felt a lightness of being, your own presence, your own energy *energizing* the room. Do you have it? Hold it there. That memory feels good, doesn't it? I wonder if you can bring that feeling into the present moment, where your connection to this infinite field of energy is unblocked, where you're not caught in fear or tripped up in your mind. You're just you, emanating light and your own authenticity. Can you get there? Right now?

Imagine how your life might expand if you could hold the feeling, the higher vibration, the higher frequency in your present life. What might you create? What might you attract into your life? What might you finish that you haven't yet started? What business would you open? What ideas could you bankroll? How might your day-to-day change, and in what ways do you want it to remain the same? Really envision it, feel into it, and write down what appears.

_____

_____

_____

_____

_____

_____

_____

_____

How do you feel? When you feel the limitless capacity within you, it's amazing how it starts to change the way you show up moment to moment. It changes how you walk into a room. It changes what you say "yes" to and what you'll no longer entertain. It changes your inner soundtrack.

Listen for the lyric of promise and possibility.

WRITE YOURSELF A CHECK

We've been talking about our relationship with money because it tends to be where people create the most resistance to receiving. For this next exercise, pull out your pen and paper and write yourself a check. On one line write "Pay to the order of" [fill in with your name] and on the line underneath it, write a dollar amount. Any dollar amount. What is the amount of money that you'd love to deposit into your bank account today? There's no right or wrong answer here; it's not a trick question. It could be any number. Once you have the dollar amount in your mind, write it down.

Did you do it?

As you hold that number in your mind, I want you to ask yourself: *Why did I choose that number?* You could have picked any number, so why did you choose the one you did? Maybe it's the dollar amount of lingering student debt you have or the amount to pay off your home mortgage. Maybe you chose the number that would pay for your kids' college tuition, or the amount you'd need to take a two-week European vacation. Maybe you chose a number that simply feels like "enough" or "plenty" or what you need to cover the basics. Whatever your number, ask yourself this: *Does it communicate limitation? An upper limit?* Think on that and we'll return to it in a minute.

– 168 –

TICKETS, TOKENS, PAPER

Most of us don't think of it this way, but the truth is that money is a neutral resource. It's not evil, corrupt, or bad, nor is it interested in one person over another. It doesn't have feelings. It's a tool of exchange that we've assigned to pieces of paper. We could have assigned it to something else, like the tokens you receive at Chuck E. Cheese or tickets at the county fair. Whether it's tickets, tokens, or green pieces of paper, money is exchanged for something of value—be it a pink stuffed panda or a service you provide. It's important to understand that money, in itself, is neutral. It's how we assign value to money that holds the charge.

When you hold beliefs such as money is hard to come by, people with money are righteous jerks, and money is hard earned, you're creating a negative charge, draining your battery. And we all know what happens when our car battery dies—it needs a positive charge to turn the engine over. Without a positive charge, your car doesn't move. It sits still, stuck, unable to move forward. Similarly, when we hold a negative charge about money, our financial life stagnates—or, worse, it suffers. Most people who struggle with money have been handed down an annoying earworm playing on repeat that they've unconsciously internalized a lyric about themselves: *I am not enough. I am not worthy.* On top of that, they've also memorized the chorus: *It's not possible, it's impossible.*

Do you know this tune? It's a very popular song, but that doesn't make it any good!

In fact, it's keeping you separate and apart from the life you really want. When you feel the emotion and low frequency of lack, of not enough, you create a negative charge within yourself that keeps you stuck in the parking lot. To become a receiver for wealth, you must increase your sense of self-worth. That is the positive charge that can help you turn the engine back on.

My friend Ramit Sethi, who wrote the book *I Will Teach You to Be Rich*, gets so fired up when people say to him, "Oh, the way to make wealth is just don't spend any money." That's ridiculous. You should be living your best life and asking yourself the questions about what really makes you happy. He created a concept called "money dials." Think of something you love to spend money on. For him, it's travel and staying in nice hotels. He tells people to think about their money dial and to turn up the dial on how much they spend on that favorite thing. How would it feel to triple, quadruple your spending on travel? Trying new restaurants? Your health and well-being? Tune into how good it feels to imagine yourself turning up the dial and allowing yourself to enjoy spending. It's energizing.

Ramit said, "Everyone teaches us how to save, but nobody teaches us how to spend. Money isn't just made to be put in a bank account. What's the point of it?" Similarly, when I ask people why they're saving, they look at me like I'm crazy. *What do you mean, why am I saving? Because you're supposed to save your money.* Okay, I say, and why? They have no answer. Their parents taught them to save, but they never taught them that money is meant to be used to create a rich life. And that a rich life can look however you want it to.

Money is a great resource, but your greatest resource is your own resourcefulness, rooted in your self-worth.

We all have the same ingredients. We're all made of the same atomic magic. We can all connect to the divine. We connect to the true source of our abundance, which is our soul. We can each choose how to perceive and become a master manifester, turning our thoughts into things.

If you make everything about money, if you view it as the end goal rather than a tool for a rich life, you are in danger of missing out on the true purpose and joy of this life. The most abundant thing is love. The richest people feel love. They are love. They give it and they get it in return. You could be a billionaire and live in an empty one-hundred-thousand-square-foot house, and you will be the poorest person. Your bills will get paid, but your soul will be empty. But the person with no money who has love to give in spades— that is truly abundant.

Here's the good news: you can fly at a different altitude that releases you from an awareness of what others have.

Money is a neutral resource exchanged for energy. People will pay a high price for things that align with the frequency of love, freedom, expansion, and joy. Furthermore, people will freely spend money on *people* who emit good vibes. When you walk into the room or show up on a Zoom call or at the podium of a conference and you're emitting the equivalent of four solid bars of 5G cell service—it doesn't really matter what you're selling—people will want it. When you are tuning into your own frequency, focusing on your own flow and energy, you will begin to attract the abundance that you crave.

Abundance is an endless frequency available to everyone. It's a birth-right available to everyone, like love and health and happiness. And money serves only as the neutral exchange of that energetic frequency, and guess what? It's everywhere! The market is swelling with trillions of dollars; there are people spending money and giving money and exchanging money all day long, all around you. Believing otherwise is to believe in fiction.

There's a beautiful teaching by the Maharal, an incredible Jewish sage who lived in the 1600s. He had an amazing metaphor about light and abun-dance. He said that a candle can light an infinite number of other candles without losing its own flame. When you come from a place of light, love, and openheartedness, there's no end to how much light you can give away. There's no end to how much you can share that light, and it doesn't diminish anything from you.

It's so powerful to realize that we have the capacity to be such a light in this world. That really is our job. We can be spreading that light in an infinite number of ways, without losing anything at all, simply creating more light.

The more we give that light to the world, the more it expands. We receive that which we give away. That's how abundance works. The more we contribute, the more we flow.

So, back to the check-writing exercise from a few pages ago. Look at the number you wrote down, and then close your eyes and take a few deep breaths. When you open them, consider that you and me and everyone on this planet has an endless capacity for compassion, empathy, and love. There's no limit to what we can give. Contrary to what most of us have been led to believe, there is no limit to what we can receive, whether that is compassion, empathy, love, or *money*. We are limited only by our limited beliefs, by our perceived limitations. The metric of the soul is infinite. So, when you assign a number or a dollar value to your worth, understand that you are placing a limit on what you will allow yourself to receive. Because the universe is tuned to the frequency of infinite expansion and abundance and there is no limited arithmetic you need to adhere to once you allow yourself to receive.

Now, pull out your pen and paper and write a *new* check to yourself. On one line write "Pay to the order of" [fill in with your name] and on the line underneath it, write a dollar amount that represents what you are available to receive this year. What is the dollar amount that correlates to possibility? Do you have your number? Did you write it down? Notice how it's different from the figure you wrote at the beginning of the chapter. Also notice how your new number makes you feel. Do you feel more willingness? Do you feel more availability? Do you feel more permission to receive? Does the number reflect a greater sense of self-worth?

Assuming your answer is "yes," that's a strong indicator you are tuning to the station of abundance.

10.

INVEST IN YOURSELF

I EXPERIENCE so much pleasure from watching women step into the most powerful versions of themselves when they allow themselves to receive. Do you feel ready to join a collective of women who are no longer holding back, who are giving themselves permission to receive abundance in their lives?

Was that a "yes"? Okay, let's freaking go!

It's time to stop shrinking and playing scared.

It's time to dream beautiful dreams and fund gorgeous projects.

It's time to be unapologetic about the musical notes within you, bursting forward to be heard and join the chorus of life. It's time to resonate at the frequency of strength, compassion, love, empathy, and courage. The universe is an intricate design of wholeness, and we're each a part of this wonderous puzzle, created to bloom fully and shine our light on the world around us.

This is your job. To bloom, to shine, to project your unique and special energy outward for all to feel, to see and hear and experience.

90 PERCENT ENERGY, 10 PERCENT ACTION

Aligning yourself with abundance requires 90 percent high-frequency energy and 10 percent right action. It's not enough to feel good—it's a *big* part of it, so do *that*—and after that, action is required.

Have you ever had a moment when you felt fiercely bold? You were just lit. There have been times in my life—like my wedding day or a big event I'm running—when I was in a peak energy state, even if I hadn't slept the night before. I could be running on two hours of sleep and no food and still feel like I was on fire creatively. I had so much adrenaline that anything put in front of me was met with "Let's do this!"

What makes somebody productive is energy. Just as our iPhones need to be charged, we, too, must be charged. And when we are charged, we are the single most powerful thing in the universe. As human beings, when we're not charged, we don't get to be conduits for the electricity. We think we're physical, but mostly we're not. We are energy beings. We are soul. We are energetic. And no matter what you want to call it, we're plugged into this Source Energy. When we plug in, we can make fire. This is why it's so important to be aligned energetically.

When your iPhone battery or your car battery dies, it needs a positive charge to turn back on or to turn the engine over. The first step to increase your charge has *everything* to do with shifting your beliefs from limitation and lack to possibility and increasing the value of your worth. From there, once your engine is running, you must shift the metaphorical car out of Park and into Drive. If you don't take this intentional action, you cannot move forward; you're still stuck in the parking lot.

You follow?

My friend and colleague Hilary Hendershott explains it this way: "As soon as you get in the right relationship with wealth, the direction of money flowing into your life will change. Before I did this in my life, the money was always going out, never coming in. And as soon as I realized that it was those strongly held beliefs from my past that were running the show, I was able to rewrite my story about money and start moving forward."

> **Money is attracted to energy
> and it responds to inspired action.**

WHAT'S YOUR NEXT RIGHT STEP?

Echoing the chorus of my favorite Tiësto song, let's get down to business! First, we must each become conscious of our unconscious beliefs about money and limitation. This is the numero uno first important step, like priming the walls before painting them. Second, and even more importantly, we must deliberately shift our energy up the radio dial. Then, to create a free-flowing channel for money, we must each take inspired action. "Money responds to commands," says Hilary. She's absolutely right, and in my experience, it also responds to a formula. Ready for it?

Formula for Manifesting Money

1. Identify your unique gift. We're going to dig into this more, but for now, your gift sits at the intersection of what you love to do, what you're good at doing, and what the world needs. This could be a service, a product, something you teach or coach about. It could also be creating an experience like an event or retreat, or creating art like books or photography. Your gift could be creating organization or beautiful design, or connection within a community.

2. Once you identify the "what," your next step is to identify the "who." Who is your audience? What sector of the population needs, craves, and is asking for what you've got? Don't you dare say "nobody" be-

cause there are people *right now* who want to pay you for your gift. There are people right now who are looking for *you*. Believe me, you're sitting on gold. Too many of us get caught up in the fear of rejection. What if they don't pick me? What if they don't like me? Those aren't helpful questions. The better question to ask yourself is, *Where am I needed today? Who can I help, serve, or uplift today?* The answer isn't "everyone"; it's a specific person, and if you think on it long enough, you'll know exactly who that is.

3. Finally, after you know the "what" and the "who," there's one last thing to do: put a price tag on it. Put yourself out into the world. Raise your hand and say, "Hi, I'm here, this is what I have to offer."

Your attention is the greatest gift you can give to someone else. Attention is a whole freaking love language. Are you speaking it? That's what people want from you—your attention. They don't care how much you know; they want to know how much you care. It's all about people. It's relationships and intimacy. It's not about numbers and sales. It's connection and communication. When you learn what's really needed you will love being in business because it's really about empathy. It works every time.

Dr. James Doty, neurosurgeon and founder of Stanford's Center for Compassion and Altruism Research and Education (CCARE), said that through the evolution of the human species, our way of thriving is by connecting to others. He said that having compassion, alleviating the suffering of others, and being present for others makes so many positive things happen to us as a by-product. He said, "It's like a virtuous cycle. When we care for others, when we're compassionate, our physiology works at its best. When we're selfish, when we're self-focused, when we want, when we feel entitled—this has all sorts of negative physiologic effects." He said if we want to be maximum manifesters, we should avoid the narrative of "I want" and instead ask, "What can I do for you?"

The answer to the questions *How can I connect with someone today? How can I change one person's world today? How can I express love, compassion, and kindness today? In a world of eight billion people, how can I serve one person today?* is the same: show up with presence. Show up as your honest, imperfect, authentic self. That's first, and that's *big*. Then when you infuse your presence into the thing you "do," whether that's baking cookies or starting a podcast, it becomes more purposeful.

We all came into this life with beautiful talents to share. And while we've all been given unique gifts, the greatest gift we've all been bestowed is presence. This is your greatest offering. So many of us get caught up with the desire to be perfect when one of the greatest acts of service that we can freely give to others is our presence—showing up as our honest, imperfect, authentic selves and holding space for another to be themselves.

SWEET SURPRISE

As you consider your unique formula for "what," "who," and "how much," I want to share a story about a woman named Mignon Francois, who is the founder and CEO of The Cupcake Collection. You may have already heard about Mignon, but you likely don't know her backstory. When she was a guest on my podcast, she told the story of driving home one day and listening to Dave Ramsey, the radio personality who offers financial advice. Mignon was broke at the time, struggling to provide for her family and to make ends meet. Ramsey said, "If you really want to make some money, have a bake sale because a bake sale is one of those things where people will give you money on the street. An honest dollar," he said, "can be earned *right in front of your house.*" And she thought, *I guess that's true.* Mignon didn't have a strong talent for baking, but she did have a box of cupcake mix in her house, and she thought, *Why not go for it?* She said to her kids, "Let's do a bake sale," and sure enough, they sold every cupcake. She turned $5 into $60 right in front of her house. Mignon told me that at that point, she decided to say "yes" to the next step. She baked more cupcakes and sold them all, turning $60 into $600. With every batch, she got better at it, and she started making money. And more money. And getting her name out there. She continued developing her recipes and eventually opened a shop. And when that shop did well, she opened another. She hired employees. Her business grew.

One cupcake box was how it all started, along with the courage to take the first step. And the icing on top was that Mignon aligned her sweet "gift" with service. She told me that every cupcake she sold was an opportunity to smile at someone, to connect with another person. And in many ways, this is what made her business so successful. In the early days, she showed up outside of busy office buildings during lunch break or in the church parking lot on Sundays. People felt her presence, her energy and warmth, and that's truly what they were buying, whether they knew it or not. She said that she started to understand that if she truly showed up for people, there was no way she could miss. "I'm so proud of what we've been able to do as a family, me and my children when we were supposed to drown, when we were supposed to be left behind. When we were supposed to continue to live in lack, continuing to want . . . *we found more.*"

During our interview, this woman thought she was telling me a story about a cupcake business, but what she was really doing was telling me and everyone listening that *you* already have what it takes. It's already in your cupboard waiting for you. If you can find the courage to make one batch, there is no telling what more you will create!

I love Mignon's story so much because at its heart it is a story about recognizing your worth and understanding that your gifts can be a blessing to someone else. When you smile or send a personal note and you show up for people, it doesn't really matter what you do; people will pay you for your presence. Because it's not about the cupcake, not really; it's about the feeling and the energy that the cupcake inspires.

WHAT DO I CHARGE?

Before we go any further, let's spend a few minutes differentiating between price and value. I see so many women I coach focused on the amount they're charging rather than the value of what they're offering. But whether we realize it or not as customers, we buy value, we buy a *feeling*, a story that has a desired vibrational frequency. It's all an energetic exchange. As Mignon's success story perfectly illustrates, if the product, service, experience, or content is valuable to someone because it makes them feel [fill in the blank with a positive feeling], then price becomes irrelevant. So, then, your substep of step 3, "put a price tag on it," is to focus on the value of what you offer people. When you infuse your presence and energy into the thing you do, whether that's baking cookies or refinishing floors, it becomes more purposeful and, thereby, *valuable*. Additionally, that thing you offer is most valuable to a specific group, often a small, niche group of people who feel seen by *you* and who recognize that you can deliver to them the thing they most value. These people are your audience.

Your job is to communicate the value of what you do.

When it comes to attaching a physical price tag to your gift, it's important to understand that payment is simply a channel for your clients and customers to receive the transformative experience they desire. What you get paid isn't really about you because they're buying a possibility for *themselves*. The action of paying means that you are letting someone else receive something they value themselves. If something was free, they wouldn't truly value it or invest themselves in using it. We must redefine how we see business and when we do it's so incredible. We can start to really serve people and be very profitable at the same time. It's great reciprocity and it's healthy for you and your customer.

I have come to think that we are often confusing false humility with true humility. Thinking that we're not enough and second-guessing ourselves doesn't make us humble. It's just a sign that we're lacking the courage to lead our way through whatever comes our way. There is so much available to us when we're willing to show up fully. By raising our hands to be there for someone else, we give others an opening to step into a new possibility. I've coached thousands of women on manifesting wealth, and on the specific subject of pricing, a large majority become uncomfortable in their seats. The primary reason for this is scarcity thinking and low self-worth, and the other is a confused notion that if you aren't undercharging, you're overcharging.

I have a few things to say about this: the market determines price, not you. You didn't decide that the current price for designer jeans should be $200. The market did. Can you find jeans for less than $200? Sure, you can find knockoff and lower-priced brands at Target, Kohl's, T. J. Maxx, and other discount stores. There is a buyer at every price. Understanding this, ask for what you're worth. End of story. When my boss at the commercial real estate company asked me, "What do you think you deserve?" I said, "$100,000." When he asked my junior colleague, Ryan, the same question, he said, "$150,000 plus double the commission." And that's what we each received. We received what we each had the courage to ask for.

We receive what we have the courage to ask for. What do you want to ask for?

When people spend money on anything, whether it's shoes or which hotel to stay at, what they're buying is a story about who they tell themselves they are. When a woman buys a pair of Jimmy Choos, she spends more because she feels unstoppable when she wears those heels. When someone stays at the Four Seasons, it's because they are choosing the identity of a person who has a certain standard of luxury. Brands and marketing are all about identity. Apple customers buy an iPad or an iMac because they want to believe in their creativity. Nike customers believe they can be the GOAT; they aren't just buying sneakers, they're reminding themselves that they can achieve greatness every time they lace up their Jordans. What we buy is about identity, and when someone spends money, they aren't making a decision about price. They spend the money on what they value, and they deeply value the stories they tell themselves about who they want to be.

As you think about the value of your work, consider that your potential client or customer is already poised and ready to spend money. If she doesn't come to your retreat, doesn't buy your scented candles or massage service, she's buying it elsewhere. You aren't saving her the $3,000 by charging less for the retreat or saving her the $35 for a candle. You're just directing her to give it to someone else, and you're unconsciously saying to yourself, *Someone else is more deserving than me.*

How does that change the way you think about your value?

When you undercharge or don't charge, you're saying, "I don't believe in creating possibility for other people." Think about it. If I didn't charge for my workshops, my retreats, or even the $30 you paid for this book, what would that say about me? I'd be unconsciously communicating that I don't think people can get well, overcome their limited beliefs, and create beautiful lives for themselves. Not attaching a dollar value to my offering can be interpreted only one way: I undervalue not only myself but also you.

If you really believe in what's possible for people, and you really believe in abundance being the way the universe works, then why wouldn't you charge for what you offer? Challenge yourself to charge an amount that requires somebody to make a deliberate decision to invest in themselves and, trust me, they will experience a more significant transformation from working with you. In fact, I challenge you to charge so much that there's charge in what you're charging. There's electricity and energy behind your price. What I've discovered is that when someone invests at a higher price point, they show up completely differently, and the type of person you attract is at a completely different level of consciousness because their energy is a match to the energy of your price point. When you charge more, when you charge what you're worth and for the *value* of what you're offering, you'll also discover that you won't need to serve as many customers, which reduces the feeling of being overworked and overstretched and increases your feeling of ease and freedom. If you undercharge for your gifts, how much can you scale? You can't. You remain a hamster on a wheel, running as fast as you can and not moving forward. And how effectively can you serve the world when you're depleted?

Invest in yourself.
Let others invest in you too.

Ultimately, it's the transaction that allows for transformation. The story of the person who spends the money is *This matters to me. I matter to me. Possibility exists for me.* Inviting people to exchange dollars for an energetic charge is priceless, so charge what you're worth and then allow people to have autonomy in regard to their choices; let them decide for themselves what they want to invest in.

WOMEN RISE UP

Once you give yourself permission to charge for that thing you do-make-create-offer to the world, you can begin to step forward into new possibilities. And not only for yourself—for women all over the world. Judaism says that money is like rain. If it falls on roses, the roses will grow. If it falls on weeds, the weeds will grow. Money energizes whatever is there. If someone has integrity and has money, they'll do more good with it. If someone is a lousy person and has more money, they'll do more harm with it. Money doesn't grow on trees or rose bushes, but it can work as an activating ingredient for good. Even Mother Teresa said it takes a checkbook to change the world. She herself raised millions and millions of dollars because she understood the power of money as a resource for good. There is a common criticism that "spiritual" people shouldn't need or want to *receive* money. Well, I will tell you that the most spiritual people I know are typically living abundant lives because their energy is dialed up; as a result, money flows to them, allowing them to live comfortably and to freely give back. You can be wired for goodness and allow money into your life. They are not mutually exclusive. In fact, they typically go hand in hand. Every hospital has names on the buildings, the funds for which were donated by wealthy people. Every theater has a name on the door, which was endowed by a philanthropic person. Every cause has been underwritten by someone with money. It is not mutually exclusive. You can be a good person and do lots of good with lots of money. I think it's past time that we normalize being wealthy and that we women—specifically—give ourselves permission to receive abundance and share it with others. Remember: creating abundance for yourself creates abundance for others. If I paint my home and make it look nicer, then I also increase the value of my neighbors' homes. We become a channel for whatever resource we receive. Think about how the money you make can flow through you and impact others in a positive way. What kind of ripple effect might you create?

CAN YOU AFFORD *NOT* TO?

When I first moved to Los Angeles in 2003, I would visit The Peninsula Beverly Hills, an exclusive five-star resort, and stay for the day. For $200, I was invited to enjoy a massage and access to the spa and pool throughout the day. My then-twentysomething friends who were also hustling for work thought I was crazy to spend the money. "What are you doing? Isn't it nineteen dollars just for valet parking?"

"Yes, but it's worth it. In fact, I can't afford *not* to do it."

They didn't understand my logic, but I understood what I was doing. I would luxuriate at the pool, feeling so good, feeling so pampered, thinking, *I belong here.* Pool attendants would come by with warm blankets that they'd tuck under my feet and cheese plates for me to nibble on. A harp player welcomed guests in the spa lobby, and after I heated up in the sauna, attendants would return and hand me iced towels smelling of eucalyptus and lavender. Throughout the day, I'd be transported to the land of possibility, to the frequency of abundance. Once a month, I treated myself in this way, and while money was tight and $200 was an expense, I didn't regard my choice as irresponsible or too expensive because by being in that environment and allowing myself to receive self-care, I was telling myself, *Here is the evidence, this reality exists. It's available to me. And I deserve it. I'm worthy of receiving it.*

This reality exists, and it's available to me.

After a day of soaking up the vibration of abundance and limitless possibility, my own inner soundtrack would change to match it, and I could almost feel myself expanding, pulsing with the music of potential. I started to train myself to tune into that frequency during my monthly spa visits and as I reclined by the pool swaying to the sound of my own good vibes, I'd receive those creative downloads I talked about earlier—ideas, insights, and inspiration that I'd take with me when I left The Peninsula and returned to "real life." Those creative insights, bought for $200, helped to inform my next step forward. In fact, it may have been while sitting at The Peninsula pool when I allowed myself to think: *If I'm not going to make records, help me see another possibility.* Underneath my dark sunglasses, I widened my internal lens to include new fields of vision, and as I made "possibility" a regular habit, I began to experience synchronicities at a pace that propelled my career forward. My spa days were a temporary drain on my bank account, but the price for not going would have been far higher.

> When you go looking for evidence
> of more possibility, you will find it.

THE COMPANY YOU KEEP

Earlier, I talked about our need to belong. It impacts what we wear, how we mow our lawn—because we don't want to violate the social norm. The social expectation drives our habits and our beliefs. This can help us form better habits and beliefs we want to have—and stick with them. While it's crucial to have a mindfulness practice and make sure you align with the divine every day, it's important to know that our beliefs and actions are also heavily impacted by the people with whom we surround ourselves. I interviewed author James Clear, who wrote *Atomic Habits*. He said that after his book came out, he realized there was something even more impactful on our ability to form habits: the people we surround ourselves with.

Think about the people you consider your close friends and family—are they living in scarcity? Or are they tapped into their own abundance and constantly tuning their dial to match that higher frequency? Every group, no matter the size, inherently has a set of established norms. James said, "You want to join groups where your desired behavior is the established 'normal' behavior. Because if it's normal in that group, then it's going to be very easy and attractive for you to adopt it because it will help you fit in. Wildly different behaviors get praised and supported and loved in different environments. If you hang out with a bunch of jazz musicians, then suddenly practicing an instrument six nights a week sounds very normal. It's really just about finding that pocket of people where you can rise together and support each other's goals and get praised for the good habit that you want to have."

If you want to start having a better relationship with money, seek out people who model a greater potential. Find people who are living with abundance and are also kind and generous. When you can reinforce a new piece of evidence in your mind over and over again, it can override that old narrative that's been driving the bus for too long.

11.

PRACTICE PURPOSE

A QUESTION OF PURPOSE

There is a prevalent new school of thought that the opposite side of the depression spectrum isn't happiness; it is *purpose*, which I define as showing up each day as our fully expressed, authentic selves and sharing our gifts in this world. I had an interesting conversation about this with Bob Waldinger, who's a professor of psychiatry at Harvard Medical School. He oversees one of the largest studies on adult life ever conducted. When they talked about happiness, the researchers asked participants, "What do you think you need to be happier?" Some people said money, others said more sleep, some believed they would be happier if they ate a healthy diet. For a week, they gave the participants the "thing" that they believed would make them happier, and at the end of the week, the finding was that nothing changed psychologically or biologically for the participants; they were the same as before. So, then, they asked them to shift their focus from what they believed would make them happier to what they believed would make someone else happier. For the next week, the participants were encouraged to give to others—small tokens of appreciation along with bigger overtures—and at the end of the week, they found that participants not only felt psychologically better but that their immunity had improved. Acting in service *changed their biology.*

I left my high-paying real estate job because I didn't feel purposeful. I didn't feel like the work I was doing reflected my creative value, nor did I feel that I was genuinely acting in service to myself or to others. That was the aha moment when *everything changed.* That was the moment when I realized that what I had to give was inside me—it was the music of my soul, and sharing my songs was the purposeful work I wanted to freely give away. Like I did, so many of us get stuck comparing our purpose with what we amass and accumulate. We evaluate how successful we are based on all kinds of ridiculous things like how many followers we have on social media, how much money is in our bank account. What if we asked ourselves a different question about what it means to be purposeful and successful? What if we asked ourselves, *How much do I value myself? What do I have worth giving? In what ways am I significant?*

I heard Oprah say once that everybody "says" they want to be successful. And, she said, the truth is that we didn't come into the world to be successful, we came into the world to be *significant.* She said she'd never met a single person who felt significant and that their life held meaning who didn't also feel successful.

We all came into this life with beautiful and significant talents to share. We *all* have been given gifts. Some people have an effortless ability to listen with their whole hearts. Others have an innate ability to motivate and inspire people. Some others can naturally create beauty with their hands while others design mathematical intricacies that help make our world work more efficiently. Whatever the gift is, every day we should ask ourselves, *How can my innate gifts be of use?*

Rabbi Aaron has a beautiful metaphor for this. He said, "Imagine you're at a construction site. And you don't know what you're doing there. Someone hands you a bag, and inside you find a saw. There's a hammer. There's a nail. Oh, I get it. I'm a carpenter. The guy next to him gets a bag. In his bag, there are testers and wires and fuses. Oh, I get it. I'm an electrician. What's in your bag?"

Rabbi Aaron continued, "But there's something else in the bag that I think is important. There's something broken in your bag. And that is so important to figure out, because what's broken in your bag is telling you where you've been trained to help others. Recently I met a woman at Shabbat who had a very abusive childhood, and she became a child psychologist. She said to me, 'Only now have I realized that had I not gone through my own trauma, I could not have helped so many children, because I wouldn't have truly understood what they were going through. And I look back now and realize that my experiences were a gift, because they have enabled me to have the capacity to be helpful to others like me.'"

He continued, "I think very often people think that the things that are broken in their bag should be discarded, that they're just trash—but there's no trash in your life, just treasures. You have to recycle the trash and turn it into treasures. We've been given strengths, but we've also been given challenges, and those challenges are just as important to figure out. The challenges or the 'problems' in your life aren't meant to be solved but rather faced. That's why it takes one to know one. And it takes one to help one."

We all have value, and we are all needed right here, right now, to play in this majestic orchestra of life, and we each have been given an instrument to play. And for every day that goes by that we *don't* feel like we are living our life on purpose—with value and significance—we suffer because we all desire to be fully expressed, to be fully found, and to fully contribute to the world.

My friend Rachel Platten is a prime example of this. She was a struggling singer-songwriter, living in NYC, not making any money, and feeling so far behind all her friends who were getting married and buying houses. Meanwhile, she could hardly afford a car. Her family didn't understand why she was still trying to chase her music dream. But Rachel just had this feeling that pushed her to keep writing and writing. Finally, at thirty-one years old, she wrote "Fight Song," but all the big labels rejected it. Some people heard it and said, "It's good," but no one really gave it a chance.

For two years the song sat in her pile of five thousand other unwanted songs. Deep down she knew "Fight Song" was meant for something bigger, so she went back to square one. She played her song at house concerts and in living rooms. She was also doing a lot of charity work in hospitals, so she would play the song for the cancer patients, and she soon recognized that the message of the song was changing people's lives. This gave her the fuel to keep going and sharing from her heart. Even after all the rejection, she thought, *I don't care. One on one, I'm making a difference.*

After a few more years of doing that, she finally had a massive spiritual awakening, of surrender. She told herself, *I am holding this dream way too tight. I am strangling the life out of it. I need it to happen so badly, I'm not even giving it room. The universe might be trying to send me things, and I am so nervous and so scared that I'm pushing them away.* So one night she fell to her knees and prayed, "God, I don't know what else you want from me. I have made music that I think will heal millions of people. I have driven around the country, I have bled for this, I have done everything. But if it's not meant to be, I accept it. If I'm just supposed to play in hospitals, that's okay." She had this feeling of "Okay, maybe the dream I've held for years is not meant to happen. And I just trust you, God. I'm putting it in your hands."

She woke up the next morning, and said to herself, *I'll never be so ego driven about this again. Who am I to say that it's not enough to play in hospital rooms and heal people? Why does my ego need to achieve something bigger?*

Then one day she was playing "Fight Song" for another group of cancer patients. A woman heard it and was so moved that she went to her brother, a production manager of a local radio station in Baltimore. She said to him, "Please put that on the radio. It's healing me. Please let other people have this power."

Within weeks, "Fight Song" became number one. Two months after that, Rachel was on stage at the Radio Disney Music Awards. Three months after that, she was on stage with Taylor Swift. Everything changed. And it was all because she showed up in service from a high vibrational energy of love, compassion, strength, and possibility in every room she walked into.

This release of ego is the key to feeling good. We each have a journey that leads us to repair whatever was once broken. The point of that path is to walk others home. Share your story and keep healing. And repeat.

So how do we each find ourselves?

First and foremost, you must clear any limiting beliefs about how you're deficient. How you're not enough, not expert enough, not ready enough, not prepared enough, not certified enough. At some point, your mind created this unconscious story; it started singing a lyric that you're not enough, that your gifts aren't valuable, that they can't be used for good. This is not true, and I encourage you to delete that song from your playlist, if you haven't already. Next, you stumble across your purpose the same way you open yourself up to receive creative downloads—by asking a new question—and in this case, I believe your purpose, whoever you are, lies at the intersection of the following four questions: What do I love to do? What am I good at? What does the world need most? And, am I willing to start messy, from wherever I am now?

Am I willing to start messy, from wherever I am now?

In doing my podcast, I've met so many people who have pursued what they loved and turned it into purpose-driven work, and they all understand that at the heart of their success is having the courage to start from a place of being messy, of being mediocre, to start as they are now and not later. When I started my podcast, I wasn't even mediocre; I was a fish out of water in a sea of thousands of already successful podcasts. What could I possibly offer? What could I possibly add that wasn't already there? I wasn't sure of my value, but I eventually allowed myself the grace to move from good intention into practice. After recording the first episode, I vowed to make at least ten more, even if they weren't very good, even if they were horrible. After those first ten, I mustered the courage to make thirty, and then fifty, and as I continued to fumble around with the mic, I got better, and eventually, I hit my stride. In fact, I hit so much of a stride that the podcast eventually took over my music career. It became *that* successful. At some point, I understood that it didn't matter if the content wasn't "perfect" because people were showing up and telling me that my authentic message resonated with them. "This is just what I needed to hear" was a frequent comment in the chat, and this helped me to understand that I was offering something that people wanted, and if I could give away a piece of my messy heart to help someone else, shouldn't I? The answer was a resounding "yes."

Howard Schultz, the former CEO of Starbucks, didn't know what intersection he would eventually stumble upon when he was a young kid, growing up poor in public housing, taking the L train to its last stop in Brooklyn. It wasn't until he was older and out of poverty and visiting Italy for work. The coffee company he was working for prior to Starbucks sent him abroad for a conference, and after days of standing in stuffy meeting rooms he decided to sneak out and see the country, and that's when he became interested in Italy's coffee culture—people frequenting espresso bars and lingering in cafés. When he returned home, he said to his wife, "I want to create a place where people come to talk to each other, to connect over a little cup of coffee." He started with a kiosk and then he built one store. He didn't start out with the purpose of creating a successful chain of thirty-five thousand stores. Rather, he tolerated his capacity to start small and let his enthusiasm and his belief in growing bigger lead him forward. His idea took years and years and years to develop.

I can't speak for Howard, but I can say that in my own life there's a heightened level of satisfaction and joy that begins to vibrate inside me when I'm developing an idea, clearing a new path, creating something out of nothing, and riding the roller coaster of life, both the high peaks and the plunging lows. There's the promise of deep fulfillment for you, too, when you stop white-knuckling your own roller coaster ride. When you let go of your tight grip and put your hands up in the air, every moment can feel exhilarating.

> You don't need to know the destination.
> You just need to follow your enthusiasm,
> follow your joy.

When it comes to taking purposeful action, start by *practicing purpose.* What do I mean by that? You can practice being purposeful by doing something that you love doing and sharing it with others. Maybe you make killer chocolate chip cookies. If that's you, bake them and share them with somebody. Maybe your act of generosity is to offer to take your friend's kids for a few hours, so that your friend can have some time for herself. Maybe it means cutting flowers from your garden and leaving them for your neighbor, or writing a sweet note that you tuck under someone's windshield wiper or into their lunch bag. If you're not sure what to do, ask someone in your life: What is something that I do well? What is something I do that brings value to your life? How do I best show up in your life? A lot of the time, what naturally connects us to others goes unnoticed to ourselves because we think that if it comes easily or naturally, then it must not be a big deal. Trust me, small things are often the biggest deals.

YOU'RE A MIRACLE

In the process of trying to get pregnant, I underwent years of fertility treatment, including a couple of rounds of IVF and several miscarriages. My doctor's office was next door to a Rite Aid in downtown Los Angeles, and for most of those years, nearly every time I went to an appointment, I'd see the same homeless man on the corner. It became my habit to give him a one-dollar bill every time I passed him on the way into the doctor's office, and he would look me in the eye and say, "Thank you; you're a miracle." After a while, I noticed that he said this to everyone who passed by, whether they gave him money or not, no matter their age, color, or socioeconomic standing. He'd look at them and deliver a heartfelt "Hey, you're a miracle."

On one particular visit to my doctor, I reached into my purse to pull out a dollar and all I had was a ten, and I thought, *Should I give him ten bucks?* And I decided, sure, yes, give him the ten bucks. So, I handed him the money and he looked at me and said, "Thank you; you're a miracle." I went into the office lobby to check in for my appointment and looked out the large glass windows that faced the street where the homeless man took his usual spot; I watched him for a minute. I watched him as another homeless man stumbled by on crutches, and I watched how he reached out to this man and handed him the ten-dollar bill I'd just given him. He pressed it into the other man's hand and said, "Hey, brother, you're a miracle."

That ten-dollar bill might have fed him for a day, and he selflessly gave it away. In that moment, I thought, *This man was the miracle.* This man was showing the rest of us what it means to have a generous heart, to show up with presence, to give freely, to express love in the simplest way.

When we act in service, when we show up for others in small and big ways, we get to practice expressing love and giving love away; we get to practice expressing kindness and compassion and giving it away, and that feels *purposeful.* Since that day many years ago, I started an intentional practice of asking myself every morning: *How can I connect with someone today? How can I change one person's world today? How can I express love, compassion, and kindness today? In a world of eight billion people, how can I serve one person today?*

Rabbi Cohen told me a story about kindness that left me in tears. In his community a few years ago, there was a terrible tragedy. A botched robbery resulted in the murder of the owner of a jewelry store. The community was traumatized, and the store was closed down. One day, Rabbi Cohen was across the street from the store and saw the son of the murdered owner opening the store. The rabbi introduced himself and expressed his condolences, and after some talking, he learned that the store was going to reopen for business.

Rabbi Cohen had the idea to rally the Jewish community to show support for this family. The day the store officially reopened, he had everybody in his community create a flash mob of kindness. He shared with me, "The widow was so overwhelmed by the act of kindness in that moment that she wrote to me months later; she's actually come to visit at the synagogue. She felt she got more support from us than from her own church, and she said the acts of kindness of the Jewish community restored her faith in humanity."

It's a beautiful testament to how we can each bring a little bit of light where there is darkness. It doesn't take much, but people's worlds can be transformed.

WHAT I'VE LEARNED is that fulfillment and purpose are the results of sharing with others, so when we hold back or resist our natural generosity and desire to connect, we feel unfulfilled. Pain isn't a by-product of what we don't have; it's the result of holding back. We are each meant to give. Another thing I've learned is that we don't give to get. We give to give. We give because it's our responsibility, our moral obligation. As Rabbi Aaron says, "We're all fixers. We've come into this world to fix what's broken within ourselves, within our friendships, within our families. There's so much that's broken within. That's what we came here to do. We came here to fix what's broken." Every one of us has been given a gift, a special talent in our lifetimes, to give away and heal that which is broken. That is the purpose of the gift.

> ## Pain isn't a by-product of what we don't have; it's the result of holding back. We are each meant to give.

Giving ten dollars to someone in need and cutting flowers from your yard to bring to your neighbor are simple gestures, and yet, they are purposeful actions. The act of doing them puts you on track to that heightened, energetic state where you begin to *receive* creative insights—whispers and clues from the universe—that nudge you to take the next step forward toward wholeness, toward balance and abundance in your own life. The good feelings that come with gestures of kindness are exactly the feelings that come when you are tuned into your frequency. The more time you spend in those feelings, the more you show up every day with presence, with good intention, and with a giving heart, the quicker the next purposeful step will reveal itself.

TUESDAYS WITH MORRIE

I interviewed the bestselling author Mitch Albom a couple of times on my podcast. I asked him how his famous book, *Tuesdays with Morrie*, all began.

When Mitch was in college, he took classes with Professor Morrie Schwartz, and they built a close bond. Their relationship developed to the point where Morrie was like an uncle. Mitch would call him "coach" and hang out at his house, and they would share meals together. After graduation, Mitch promised he would stay in touch—but of course, life got in the way for the next sixteen years and Mitch never contacted him. He was busy getting into the music business and then the sports journalism world, eventually landing an ESPN radio show.

As he tells it, "One night, I happened to be flipping the remote control. And there he was: Morrie was on the *Nightline* program talking to Ted Koppel about what it was like to be facing a terminal illness.

"I decided I would call him up. That was all it was going to be, and then I'd go back to my busy life. It was the nurse who answered the phone, and she handed it to him. And I remember exactly what I said. 'Hello, Professor Schwartz. My name is Mitch Albom; I was a student of yours in the seventies. I don't know if you remember me.' And the first thing he said to me after sixteen years was, 'How come you didn't call me coach?' By the end of the conversation, I planned to go to visit him, because guilt is a very powerful motivator."

Mitch went to see Morrie, thinking it would be a one-time thing. He didn't expect what he would see there. "I was just so taken with the way he was handling his dying from Lou Gehrig's disease and the fact that he couldn't move his legs and could barely move his arms at that point and he knew he was going to die, but he was still so vibrant and had so much to say, so much that he was still interested in. And I remember going home that night, thinking to myself, *You're thirty-seven years old, you're perfectly healthy, and he's seventy-eight years old and dying. And he seems ten times more content and happy with his life than you are with yours. There's something to learn here.* So, I began to visit him every Tuesday and one after another after another after another. It turned out to be all the Tuesdays that he had left in his life. And we kind of did this last class together on what's really important in life once you know you're going to die, and wouldn't it be great to have that knowledge when you're young and healthy, when you can still change your life and do something about it?

"The book came about when he told me one day that he was afraid that he was going to die twice. And I asked, 'What does that mean?' And he said, 'Well, first I'm going to die when I die. And then I'm going to die a second time when my family has to sell the house to pay all the bills I've accrued for years by dying slowly. We don't have the money to pay for it.' It was then that I got the idea: maybe I could write a book to help him pay his bills. And I didn't tell him that I was going to try to do that. Because I was afraid that if I promised that and then I failed to sell it, I would just make his life worse. So, I privately went to different publishers in New York and said to them, this is kind of an amazing story about a man who is dying talking to a young man about what matters in life." Mitch said that he told the publishers that he didn't need a lot of money, and he gave them the exact amount he needed to help Morrie get out of debt.

"Everybody said no," he said. "No one was interested. They said it was boring, depressing, that nobody's going to want to read a book like that. One very prestigious publishing house told me that I didn't know what a memoir was and I should come back in twenty years. I really would have given up, to be honest, if it was for me. I would have thought, *Forget it, I'll go on to something else.* But because it was for somebody else, which is a lesson in and of itself, I pushed harder, and I finally found a publisher who was interested in it. And we were able to come to an agreement.

"I went to Morrie and told him, 'Hey, all these conversations we're having—well, there's a publisher who wants to turn them into a book. And not only that but they're going to give us some money. I want you to take all the money and pay off your medical bills so you don't have to die twice.' Committing to do this had no promise for me. I just wanted to be a sportswriter. And I thought, *This is going to take me some time to go off into left field and write this, but it's worth doing because I can help him.*

"I wrote it as simply as I could, without a lot of embellishment. And I didn't start writing until after Morrie died, and I really tried to keep it simple.

"Then a funny thing happened. People began to read it. It came out in August of 1997 and didn't show up on a bestseller list until November, and it didn't reach the top of any lists until April of the following year. It was a slow process of people passing it around. And its success changed my life. I haven't written a sports book since.

"As John Lennon famously said, 'Life is what happens to you while you're busy making plans.' My plans [before Morrie] were something different from the plans that the world had for me."

PRACTICING PURPOSE

The wonderful thing about practicing purpose is that it doesn't matter what you practice. It's about allowing yourself to simply start. Being mediocre doesn't matter. It's about doing something that excites you in its imperfect form.

Can you imagine doing that?

And then, from there, can you imagine giving it away?

Before you answer, I want you to think about the last time you experienced something you loved. Maybe it was a great book or movie. Maybe it was a piece of music, an art show, or a new neighborhood you recently discovered in your own town or city. Maybe it was as simple as returning to your favorite flavor of ice cream. Think about what you did immediately afterward. You wanted to share it, didn't you? You wanted to text a friend or turn to your partner and say, "Hey, you have to read this book! See this movie! Try this ice cream!" When we experience love and compassion, creativity and connectivity, or the simple and raw feeling of joy, our natural inclination is to share it. So then, imagine what it could feel like if you gave those pieces of yourself away.

Imagine sharing yourself. Unfiltered. Unapologetic.

And then, imagine if, after showing up again and again and again, you woke up on the other side of mediocre? What if what you start *today* is the first step toward a more purposeful life, one where you show up every day as your fully expressed, authentic self and where you freely share your love and kindness, compassion, and creativity with the world? How would that change your life? How would that change the world? I'll tell you—it would change the world in a masterful way.

12.

FIND YOUR CONFIDENCE

As you think about stepping forward into the world and sharing your gifts, you may feel uncomfortable. Maybe really uncomfortable. This is normal. Stepping forward and out of your familiar routine can bring discomfort, and this is typically an unconscious reaction to an experience in your past. As we begin this chapter, take a moment to step back in time. Can you recall something that happened in your early life where you didn't get the approval that you desired? Maybe it was trying out for the baseball team, and you didn't get picked to play. Maybe your art teacher nodded her disapproval and suggested you focus your "creativity" elsewhere. When I was in high school, I auditioned for every school musical and never got a part, not one solo line. The theater director explained it this way: "You might be able to sing, but you can't dance, and you need to be good at both to make it in musicals."

Ouch.

Whether we're consciously aware of it or not, as we confront new challenges or consider expressing a new piece of ourselves in the present, we tend to play back disappointing moments from the past like a song on an old record album. This song of insecurity and doubt that was hardwired into our central nervous system long ago is the song of the small self who believes it should only do things it is really good at doing. The small self resists mediocre. It wants to be good, really good, an expert and maybe even perfect—right now. The small self is overconcerned with perfection, performing, and pleasing, while the Soul self is simply thirsty to serve, to express itself freely.

BE MORE LIKE A DOLPHIN

One of my favorite places to visit is South Carolina, and this past summer I took my family to stay at the gorgeous Montage Palmetto Bluff nestled along the May River. This spectacular landscape feels otherworldly with its ancient live oak trees draped in moss and the fresh salt air that hangs heavy and fills one's lungs. One afternoon, we drove down to the coastline and swam with dolphins in the Atlantic Ocean. It was exquisite. The dolphins were so majestic, so naturally graceful. At one point, back in the boat, I turned to Lowell and said, "Just look at those dolphins. They're in flow. The water moves, they move. They move, the water moves. It's an effortless dance. There is no withholding. You can almost see the energy flowing through them, giving energy to the ocean as they swim through it."

We could all learn a thing or two from the dolphins.

Number one: when you express yourself authentically, without withholding, you are a gift to the world, a beauty to behold.

Number two: you are ready to swim. Right now.

I hear resistance to that second part constantly in my work. "But I have to be someone better first" is what people often say to me when I drop these points on a coaching call or at a retreat. "Cathy, I'm not ready yet." "I still have work to do." "If I put myself out there now, I'll be panned. I'll be made a fool." "I have to wait."

Wait for what? The master plan? The master's degree? The masterpiece?

A few years ago, I interviewed Malcolm Gladwell, author of five *New York Times* bestsellers and best known for his brilliant insights into human psychology, sociology, and popular culture. In our interview, he talked about his background in journalism, his early reporting on business for the *Washington Post*, and how it was his curiosity and not his credentials that led him down the path of studying human behavior. I remember thinking, *Hey, wait a minute, Malcolm was a journalist first, and not a scientist?* And then following that thought with another—*What a shame it would have been if he'd said to himself before writing* The Tipping Point: *Who am I to do this?* If he would have stopped himself because he didn't have the degree, wasn't expert enough, or wasn't ready yet, the world would have been denied his groundbreaking ideas.

You don't need to be more to get started.

My friend Deborah is a successful screenwriter, and she said something to me that I'll never forget. She said, "There's only one thing you have to do to make the audience hate a character, to stop rooting for them. Do you know what it is?"

"I don't know," I admitted.

"Make the character perfect. If the character is perfect, by the end of the first act, the audience will turn on that person; they will have no sympathy for them, and likely no interest."

"Interesting," I said. "So then, what makes a character lovable?"

"Flaws. A character who messes up and can laugh at themselves or can keep going despite their imperfections will have the audience rooting for them all the way."

I thought about this in the context of the podcast I started eight years ago. I told you that when I started, I wasn't even mediocre. I was a novice, a newbie. And I remember sitting in my small closet poised to record my first episode. My linen closet with the accordion doors was the only place I could find in my house that was quiet and hidden from children, and so I folded myself into the cramped space and I pressed Record. Six hours later—thanks to my husband, who'd taken full control of the household and our children—I was still at it, sitting in the dark, under a shelf of towels. Nothing I'd recorded sounded quite right. I didn't like the sound of my voice, and after six hours, I was tired and hoarse. I started crying, berating myself for being "so bad at this," and for ignoring my family at the expense of what? Another podcast in a sea of thousands. I sat on the floor of my closet and allowed my thoughts to run wild—*I'm not doing this. Who am I to do this? I don't know who I am thinking I can do this. I don't have any listeners. I don't have a social media presence. I don't even have an email list. I'm not a famous person. I'm foolish. I'm a fake. I'm an imposter.* As I continued to sit there, allowing the weight of comparison and self-doubt crush me, I sent a text to Emma, the podcast producer I had just hired: I changed my mind. I'm not going to do the show.

The following day, I received a call back from Emma, who suggested that I "just try it and see how it goes." I thought, *Clearly this woman has not heard the six-hour disaster I recorded in my linen closet,* and yet her words stuck with me: just try it and see how it goes. I rolled her words around in my mind all day and they pushed up hard against my small self, the imposter, who returned: *You're not ready. You're no good at this.* Back and forth, my mind went until I realized that I was making the podcast all about me. What if I refocused on the people I wanted to reach and help? I thought, *What if there's one person today whose life might be touched by something I have to say?* By the end of the day, I relented. *Maybe I'll just see how it goes.* I allowed myself the grace to try it again, and today, the podcast based on the premise that anyone can free themselves from the patterns that hold them back from possibility has over 50 million downloads. We've done more than nine hundred episodes. I've grown in countless ways. My daughters see a world of possibility. I'm so grateful I didn't listen to that voice in my head that said *You're not ready; no one will listen; it's too hard.* The experience has changed my life in such a profound way.

I've thought about that pivotal moment many times since then: What if I had made that one tiny decision to not continue to do my podcast? I would have missed out on growing as a person. I would have missed out on meeting so many amazing people and propelling my career. So many doors that opened as a result of taking Emma's advice would have remained shut. The moral of the story is to stop overthinking it. Imagine what could happen if you had the courage to just begin.

Too many of us stop ourselves from showing up because we don't want to appear messy and imperfect, but like my friend Deborah pointed out, nobody likes a perfect person. It's hard to root for and relate to perfection. The relatable person is the one who sits on the floor of her closet and lets her heart out, because guess what? There are many others like her, who know every inch of their own closet and who can commiserate: *I get you; I've been there. And I've found a way out.* I'm so thankful that I pressed publish on that first episode before I was "ready." I'm so glad I didn't wait or continue to convince myself that I needed to be an authority, an expert, or more credible before I allowed myself to move forward. I understood that I didn't need to be more before I started. Neither do you. You don't need all the answers. You don't need to prove yourself. You're already good enough.

We build this expectation that "If I'm not perfect and if I create something that's not perfect then it's not worth trying." How ridiculous is that? Perfectionism is just a trauma response. When Harry Connick Jr. was a guest on my podcast, he shared something he tells his daughters who are also musicians: "Give yourself something to edit." The first draft is never going to be perfect.

I want you to be a C student with something to edit. I want you to be willing to be mediocre, willing to let go of the shame. You're not going to get it all right away. None of us do. If you allow yourself to be a C student and you let that be enough, you're going to go so far.

TUNE OUT THE SMALL SELF

The small self is overconcerned with perfection, performing, and pleasing. The small self, albeit small, is extremely loud. The small self is like the static on the radio station that makes it nearly impossible to hear the music of the soul. The good news is that clearing the static is always only one breath away, so when you find yourself getting stuck, feeling competitive and small, employ your meditation practice. Close your eyes and put your hand on your heart. Take a deep breath in and out and bring your awareness to the present moment. Observe your thoughts. Become curious about them. What are they saying? Are they true? When your small self says, "I am not ready; I am not enough," push back.

When I was gearing up to interview Matthew McConaughey on my podcast, even though I'd been hosting the show for almost four years at that point, my small self started in, talking very loudly: "Who am *I* to interview Matthew McConaughey? In the context of Matthew McConaughey, I'm irrelevant; I am not worthy." My small self reminded me how famous he was, how handsome and wealthy he was, and how I—little Cathy Heller—had much less to bring to the table. I started to spin and before I spun out, I put my hand on my heart and closed my eyes and I told my small self to stop telling me lies. I invited my brighter presence forward and it whispered: "Let's just do this thing. Let's meet; let's hold presence; let's connect." And this is how I changed the dial.

When Matthew appeared on my screen, smiling widely back at me, I said, "Before we begin, I just have to say—you are so hot, you are so hot, you are so hot! I'm barely breathing, and I just have to say it out loud. I'm dying here. Okay, now that I've said it, we can move on."

My silly admission was exactly the icebreaker I needed to lower the pressure and anxiety of performing. Plus, he laughed, and that relaxed me even more. For the next hour, we talked about his new book, *Greenlights*, and his own reservations about starting something new. He opened up about his desire to be known for himself—Matthew, the person—apart from his acting roles. It was an intimate and honest conversation, and we ended up talking an extra half hour longer than we were supposed to. It was one of my favorite interviews, too, because, duh, it was Matthew McConaughey, and because it reinforced something I already knew but that my small self had tried to make me forget: honesty and authenticity create openings for connection. And presence reinforces connection. When we make space for people, when we meet them with an open heart and give them the gift of our presence, without withholding, without editing ourselves, we create connection.

When we bring presence to what we do, it becomes more purposeful.

YEAH, BUT...

So often I hear people say, "Yeah, but I'm still not ready . . . " "I'm not good enough yet . . . " "I still have work to do." We can trick ourselves into thinking this is humility, but it's nothing other than fear. And self-doubt. And these things will hold you back. They will distract you, keep you small, keep you quiet.

If you haven't already, it's time to change your internal lyrics to:

I am ready now. I am enough now. I am worthy now. I am already a masterpiece.

No "yeah, buts"! Arm yourself with a little courage and go!

When it comes to setting down perfectionism and self-doubt, I hear so many people say, "I just need more confidence." I'm here to tell you that courage comes first. Courage means being scared and doing it anyway. The more we paint, the more we drive, the more we write, the more we parent, the more we gain confidence. But courage comes before confidence.

Confidence is learned through courage. When you see a kid learning to walk, they're just going on courage. They fall a bunch of times, and then they start to get more and more confident because they've done it, and they are learning that they can get back up and try again. A helpful reminder for us adults is this: your soul, the mystical part of who you are, is way more interested in the feeling that comes when you're scared and doing it anyway. That's the best satisfaction. And the more you do the scary thing, the more you'll likely start looking for something new to challenge you, to give you those butterflies, because it's the best feeling of satisfaction to go beyond your limit, to do something that stretches you. If it's easy, you won't experience that elated feeling of *Oh my God, I just pushed past my upper limit.*

It's also important to remember that whatever you're growing toward—whether you're raising your price, setting a new boundary, or showing up with more authenticity—whatever it is that stretches you today is something that you once believed was off-limits, that you couldn't do that because it wasn't safe, it was too scary. But actually scary is good, because you're going beyond the reef. You're going further than what you've told yourself you can do. That's why it's so exhilarating. It's like watching my daughter the first time she went on Thunder Mountain at Disneyland after refusing to go on it in the years before. There finally came a time when she said, "I'm going on this ride." She was so proud of herself. That feeling of doing something she thought she couldn't do was better than the feeling of being comfortable.

Author Bob Goff said to me on my podcast that it takes only twenty seconds of courage to change your life. If you had twenty seconds of courage today, twenty seconds to lean in and show up for yourself and to show up for others, your entire day would change. Twenty seconds of raw courage could put you on the path to a new destination.

You have a greater capacity for courage than you often know. We easily get defeated, but we can cultivate grit. The fastest way to do this is in practicing optimism, repeating affirmations. Select your thoughts the way you select your clothes for the day. "It's here. It's working out. I'm enjoying this process. I appreciate how much fun the adventure is. I love how much I learn about myself through this process. Life is truly amazing. There are miracles all around me all the time."

WHAT PSYCHOLOGIST and bestselling author Angela Duckworth's research has taught us about grit is that it directly correlates to optimism. Most gritty people, it turns out, are optimistic. You can't cure cancer if you're not optimistic. You cannot go to a lab every single day for thirty-five years and say, "We still don't have a cure. I am defeated." Imagine if Jonas Salk, who developed a successful vaccine for polio, had had that attitude. You've got to be gritty. And to be gritty, you have to say, "I know it's here. I know it's coming." And it will, and that's for anything you do. That's why I love watching people take on new challenges, because it will reveal where they have grit and where they bow out of their lives. None of us can afford to bow out. You've got to be gritty in your day-to-day life. In your business, in your marriage, in your growth, in anything that could push you past your comfort zone.

We get in life what we have the courage to ask for.

Most of us overestimate what would need to happen for us to have a more abundant life. We underestimate how much we could create by simply showing up, by following our curiosity. By engaging in life without worrying or trying to second-guess the outcome. I want to let you in on a little secret: the people who are rewarded disproportionately in life have the courage to be messy, to start before they're "ready." When I posted on Instagram "In life, we get what we have the courage to ask for," the response was overwhelming. One woman replied, "I always thought you get what you get." Another said, "I was taught that I only get what I deserve." My response was, "You deserve it all, and the question is, do you have the courage to ask for it? What might you *do* if you could muster twenty seconds of pure courage? If you allowed yourself to be optimistic? Would you send the text, write the first page of your book, sign up for the class? Would you walk outside and take the first steps toward the marathon you've been wanting to run? If there was no perfectionism, no withholding, no failure, no judgment, what would you do *today*?

COURAGE OVER CONFIDENCE

Ask yourself: *What might I do if I could muster twenty seconds of pure courage?* If you weren't letting fear get in the way, what would you do?

_____

_____

_____

_____

_____

Of the things you wrote down, which one gives you the chills? Makes your heart pound a little harder? The things that scare you from a place of exhilaration are indications of where your soul is asking you to have courage. Believe it or not, our unconscious self—our Soul self—wants to push past barriers. It wants to be challenged and even to be uncomfortable. One of my daughter's favorite movies is the Disney movie *Moana*; it's about a young girl who longs to leave her Hawaiian island and venture beyond the reef and explore the open water.

We all want to go beyond the reef. We all want to push past our fear and discover what lies beyond. What's calling you?

If I'd never had a baby or wrote music or started a podcast, I would not have experienced how much more is *out there*. Fear can talk us out of anything and everything, so the challenge is to listen to what calls us and then bravely and boldly step toward it. With each step forward, you surrender fear and then there's no telling how far you'll go.

If there's nothing on your calendar that scares you a little bit, you won't grow, and your soul craves growth. What you truly want is the feeling and the knowing that you found within yourself the capacity to go beyond what you thought was your limitation. You might not think you do, but your soul wants to go beyond the reef, and when you do, when you set down your doubts and courageously show up with authenticity and presence, the universe opens up a channel— directly to you—for receiving. Opportunities will begin to unfold, and not because you're confident *yet*, but because you are available. Not because you're confident *yet*, but because you are optimistic. Not because you're confident *yet*, but because you are courageous.

13.

CREATE IN THE MOMENT

A S YOU GIVE YOURSELF the space to be present, you will tap into the frequency of abundance through your own *creativity*. A lot of us have learned to mistake the term *creativity* as being limited to visual and theatrical arts like dancing or painting, but creativity is broader than "art." It's also much simpler. Creativity is seeing something in a new way, it's a new *thought*. And not the cortisol-inducing kind that creates anxiety but rather a high-conscious thought that can be best heard in the pause between the notes. Creative thoughts are found in the present moment, when you're *being* rather than doing. It's often associated with spontaneity. We've spent a lot of time talking about the radio dial because in order for us to allow for the creation of abundance, our energy has to be tuned to the frequency of the moment. To access the ideas, impulses, and synchronicities that will lead us in beautiful new directions, we must create from a place of *be-ing*. This is our opening to receive.

We are all here to create.

Creativity can be a hot-button topic because a lot of people, maybe even you, don't believe in their inherent creativity. Make no mistake: we are all creators, and we are all here—in this lifetime, in this moment—to create. On my podcast, I asked Julia Cameron, who wrote *The Artist's Way*, whether she believes that everyone is creative, and she said, "Have you ever been in a preschool and seen a child who's not creative?"

The answer is obvious. Every child is creative. I thought about my own kids, who love to build forts in the backyard, who will spend an hour making dance videos, beading bracelets, or playing endlessly with slime, that stuff that ruins the couch (they love it!). As children, most of us were naturally creative—willing to get paint in our hair and sand up our noses—but as we got older, somebody came along and shattered our heart, our belief in our inherent creativity, and because we want so badly to belong, we listened to them and turned down our own voice.

GET CREATIVE

It can be helpful on your journey to embracing your true creative power to notice what messages you received about creativity as you were growing up. Grab a pen and paper and respond to these prompts. What do you notice about the messages about creativity that you may have unconsciously embraced?

My dad's view on/experience with creativity was _____

_____

_____

_____

_____

CREATE IN THE MOMENT

My mom's view on/experience with creativity was

_____

_____

_____

_____

_____

_____

In my childhood home, creativity was regarded as/talked about as

_____

_____

_____

_____

_____

For all the difficulty I had growing up, there was a lot of beauty too. There is always a mixture of things in every family. My mom had high highs and low lows. When she was feeling good, she was a lot like Peter Pan. She would let me eat dessert for dinner, encourage me to skip school to join her for a beach day, and stay up late to watch *The Honeymooners* and *Your Show of Shows* till one in the morning. My mom celebrated creativity, and I was encouraged to enroll in art and dance classes. I also played piano and took voice lessons and had a craft corner in my room for collage projects where I stuck glitter to glue, along with found objects like beads, shells, and feathers. I loved these activities because they were fun—and more than that, they opened up and released a feeling within me of freedom and beauty. My "art" connected me to something more. A current of

- 215 -

energy that inspired me in the moment and nudged me forward. I quickly observed that this experience was not shared in many of my friends' homes. Most of my childhood friends complained of being pushed academically by their parents, who believed that achievement was more valuable than play. One of my best friends from high school wanted to be in theater; her parents called it a "frivolous" use of her time and pledged that they wouldn't pay her college tuition if she enrolled in any theater productions. This friend pursued a career in accounting. She followed the path her parents pushed on her, the less creative one, and received her MBA. The last time I saw her, she admitted to being unhappy. "I'm forty-five," she said, "and I still dream of the theater."

This is a far-too common story, and a regrettable one, because all of us are creative beings, and there's a way in which we can each add something to the people in our lives, our communities, and the planet when we start to understand how much creativity we can each tap into, from frequency alone, from the simple joy of the present moment. Despite what you learned growing up, a creative life is not reserved for only a few. It is available to everyone.

SWAMP OR PARK?

There's a famous story about Walt Disney in a helicopter, flying over thousands of acres of swampland in Anaheim, California, in the early 1950s, when he turned to the copilot and cried, "Do you see that?" The pilot said, "No, Mr. Disney, I just see miles of swampland." And Walt said, "Look again, look again. I see it—I can see the balloons, I can hear the music on Main Street. We're going to make this place. We're going to build it."

Disneyland began as a thought that Walt Disney permitted himself to have without dismissing it, overediting it, or overthinking it. He allowed himself a creative thought that he built on, and on and on and on, and you can feel the journey of his unharnessed creativity when you're in the theme park. It's woven throughout the music, it's in the fireworks shows and the parades. It's evident in the joy and exhilaration of every ride and in the smiling faces of every child. Disneyland is a creative thought that was allowed to fly free.

We each have the capacity to create and build worlds, to turn thoughts into things.

But . . . Walt Disney was a visionary, a larger-than-life personality whose ideas and creativity went far above and beyond what the rest of us can create. Is that what you're thinking? What if I told you that the only difference between you and Walt is that you aren't open to your own creative impulses because you don't know where they will lead? You can't see the park beyond the swamp, and so you stop yourself before you allow your creativity to speak.

WHAT'S STIRRING IN YOUR SNOW GLOBE?

Imagine that I've just handed you a snow globe. As you shake it, I want you to imagine that the snow represents all the conscious and unconscious feelings inside you. Those feelings generate flurries of thoughts, and when there's enough momentum behind the flurry, it becomes a blizzard. In other words, a recurring thought will capture your attention. You will become aware of it as if it's swirling right in front of you. And then what happens? What does everyone do once they have a clear thought driven by a clear feeling? They act on it. They say something, they do something, they move somewhere, they break up with someone, they sell the house, they sign up for the marathon or the French cooking class.

You with me so far?

We are each creating snow flurries from our feelings and thoughts every day. And that's okay, so long as we understand what we're stirring up. If the scene in your snow globe isn't beautiful, if it's not magical and something you enjoy looking at, then you are stirring up unconscious and repetitive low-energy vibrations in your life. For example, you find yourself in the same unfulfilling relationship or job and you wonder, *How did I get here again?*

Take a moment now and look into your imaginary snow globe. What's in there? Is it a swamp, or can you see your own amusement park? We each have the capacity to create and build worlds, to turn thoughts into things. And the most magical worlds are created by inspired thoughts, the ones that we allow ourselves to become curious about in meditation or yoga class or when we're walking barefoot through the grass. These thoughts and feelings aren't necessarily devoid of sorrow or pain, of frustration or loss. The differentiator is that they are absent of judgment. They are aligned with authenticity, with what feels *true*.

That said, we can have thoughts that feel true but still lead us back to the swamp. So, ask yourself: *Does my recurring flurry of thoughts inspire possibility or does it spin me down into limitation and lack?* Awareness allows for creation. It allows you to create intentional worlds. The world of your dreams.

Become aware of what's in your snow globe, and if the scene isn't pleasing, then create a new flurry of feelings and thoughts. How do you want to feel? What do you want to see? Is it cozy? Is it settled? Is it peaceful? Is it abundant? Is it expansive? Is it loving? The more you can conjure an awareness of the feelings you desire, the more the thoughts will follow. And your thoughts can inspire your best creations.

When I was a kid, I loved to watch the show *Rainbow Brite*, an animated series about a young girl who used her magic belt to protect the colors of Rainbow Land. She also had this trick where she would open a door, and instead of finding a room on the other side of the door, a rainbow would greet her and lead her to some magical thing. I loved this concept so much that, at six years old, I would walk through my darkened house and close the doors to my and my sister's bedrooms, my parents' bedroom, and even the bathroom. I would close every single door, and then I would proceed to open them all slowly, hoping for a rainbow on the other side.

I did eventually find the door that led me to a more colorful life, and that is because I learned to become conscious of my feelings and to intentionally shift them up the dial where they could create a flurry of magical thoughts that inspired new dreams.

MIND CONTROL

We've talked about our culture's love affair with control and predicting outcomes, and what did I tell you? Our thoughts are the only thing we really have any control over. When you allow for creative thoughts, it's amazing what comes through, and not only for you but also for the people around you—because creative thoughts are vibrations that uplift those around you. When you allow space to receive impulses, synchronicities, and ideas, not only will you have more fun but also you will be led in the direction you're meant to go. You will receive the right answer. It's that simple. Give yourself permission to receive.

Not every one of my retreats goes off without a hitch. Every so often, and inevitably, someone will shoot up their hand and say, "Cathy, I don't care about all this talk about creativity and allowing for 'abundant thoughts'; just tell me how to make money." I love this because this *is* how you make money. Creativity is how you make it. When you allow for creative thought, abundance can't miss you because it's on the other side of creativity. Money never comes first; creativity leads. The creative idea of Tesla or Sesame Street came first, and the money followed. All the things you spend money on are the product of someone's creative vision.

MY FRIEND CHRISTINA Perri, like me, moved to Los Angeles to become a songwriter. For months, she waited tables during the day and tried to break into the club scene at night. Nothing was happening. Finally, she called her parents and said, "I'm coming home." She started packing up her apartment, including her beloved *Twilight* series book covers that she'd framed and hung on her walls. The next morning, Christina received a call from a friend who'd just suffered a breakup. She said to Christina, "Please come over and sing for me. That will cheer me up." Christina took a break from packing to attend to her brokenhearted friend. The original song she sang that morning her friend later posted to YouTube, where it went viral. Guess what happened next? Singer Jason Mraz's manager saw the video and reached out to Christina. Within five months, she played her first three live shows on *CBS Morning Show*, *The Tonight Show with Jay Leno*, and *So You Think You Can Dance*. Atlantic Records asked her to write a song for the new . . . wait for it . . . *Twilight* movie. Coincidence, or creativity at work?

When we allow our creativity to flow and fly free, when we give ourselves permission to say "yes," our creative capacity expands so much wider than we could have imagined. Like Christina, I came to LA thinking I would get a record deal. But once I stopped trying to force my vision and began asking a new question—What if there is another way to get my music into the world?—I received a new creative thought. That thought led me in the direction of writing music for TV, and then another thought led me in the direction of creating a podcast, and then another thought led me to the idea of creativity retreats, and every step of the way, money has followed my thoughts. The creative thought always comes first.

ASK A NEW QUESTION

One of the best ways I know of to start receiving creative downloads is to ask a new question. What would be the most fun way to live my life? How could I have more ease? What if I made joy a priority? What lights up my heart? What type of people do I want to surround myself with? What is the best way for me to serve the world?

Amy Purdy was an avid snowboarder who lost both her legs to meningitis. Her doctors weren't sure she'd ever walk again. In fact, they were shocked she'd even survived her illness, but Amy had different ideas, and top of mind was that she wanted to learn how to snowboard with two prosthetic legs.

The first time she got up on a snowboard, her prosthetic legs came off. She had a moment of either saying, "Forget it, this will never work" (which is what the chorus of "professionals" around her were saying) or asking a new question: "What if I'm the first person to figure out how to do it?" She decided to go with the latter, and so she began to meet with engineers who might be able to help her create feet that could move and bend mechanically, the same way that flesh and bone feet do. And guess what? They created her vision, and those feet are showcased in the Smithsonian now. By building on a series of questions that inspired creative thought, Amy created a category in the Special Olympics for people with prosthetics who snowboard. She then went on to win the Paralympics three times, becoming an inspiration to people all over the world. Since she first took to the snow on her prosthetic feet, thousands of people like her with disabilities have learned how to snowboard.

Our capacity to create is much bigger than we think it is, and our destiny is so much more magnificent than what we envision for ourselves. Every billion-dollar idea originated as a creative thought, and it likely came from a question—How can I solve this problem? How can I do this differently? What more is possible?

TOLERATE THE PROCESS

Does the first creative thought immediately lead to the billion-dollar idea, to the Olympic win, to life-changing impact?

No. Not usually.

It's a process.

It's a matter of degrees.

And it requires tolerance and trust.

In a painter's studio, you'll find paint everywhere. In a musician's band room, you might stumble on a mess of instruments out on the floor, and on my writer's desk, there are scribbles of notes everywhere. For creativity to run free, there needs to be a tolerance for the process, a patience for the unpredictable and unimaginable. So many of us have bought into this limited idea of the universe, of our place in it and of what we are capable. When we discard this limitation, we're able to broaden the lens on the movie of our life to see that the universe is constantly moving us forward in a direction of wholeness. My favorite story to illustrate this point is the story of Nelson Mandela. During his time in prison, unable to imagine that his circumstances could get any worse, he allowed a new thought: *What if I could get out of here?* And from the creation of that question, he created another: *How would I do that?* And then, inspired by that question, he started writing letters to the US government, asking for help. And then he started thinking, *What if they come through? What if they get me out of here?* And then he asked, *And if they do, how will it be better? The state of my country is the same as when I was put behind bars. Who's going to run my country?* And then he had another new thought: *What if it's me?* The rest is history—Nelson Mandela was freed and became one of the most influential leaders of a democratic South Africa and a figure of freedom throughout the world. And it all began as a series of creative thoughts, of opening up to what more was possible.

We get what we expect, so we each ought to expect miracles. Sure, we can remain inside the perimeters of a 3-D life that's controlled and predictable—or we can make ourselves available for something so much bigger, better, brighter, and more exciting when we allow for a thought that carries a whisper of possibility. If you can catch that thought in midair, the next thing you know, you hear another whisper—of an idea, this time. *Wouldn't that be cool?* or *I'm going to call so and so* or *Maybe I should do this.* It's in the space between the notes—the creative thought, the idea, the inspiration, the nudge—and once you allow yourself to listen, the space expands. It grows. It allows for new questions: What else is possible? Where might I be led today? What clues are around the next corner, or right here in front of me, that may lead me toward wholeness and abundance? Take a chance. Act on a hunch. And as you start to feel how wide open and infinite the space is, and as you allow more creative thoughts to come through, just watch what happens next.

14.

BE A RECEIVER

ONLY SIX MONTHS into hosting my podcast, I was invited to go to a podcast conference in Anaheim called Podcast Movement. I was new to the medium and still feeling a bit like a fish out of water, but I thought, *Why not? It might be interesting.* So, I went, and on day one of the conference, I walked into this huge hotel lobby packed with people, the volume of voices near a fever pitch. I turned to my producer, Emma, and said, "The energy in here is frenetic. What's going on?" I noticed clusters of people around the room, leaning into each other, literally rubbing elbows and exchanging tiny pieces of paper. "What are they doing?" I asked her.

She smiled knowingly. "They're exchanging business cards."

I looked at her. I didn't bring business cards. I don't even have business cards. "Remind me why people do this."

Emma smiled again. "They're trying to network, to meet people and pitch their podcasts." She lowered her voice. "Although the person they all want to meet is the head of Apple Podcasts, because that's how they'll get the most listeners. Something like seventy-five percent of podcast listeners listen to Apple Podcasts."

"Is that so?" I looked around the room again, feeling the desperate, exhaustive energy swirling around me. "I can't do it. I'm out." I turned to leave the room.

"Where are you going?" Emma asked.

"Somewhere quiet where I can ground and center. I'll catch up with you for the first panel."

I left the main lobby, walked out the front door, and wandered into the adjacent hotel a swimming pool's distance away. Inside this lobby, it was quiet and calm, and I promptly sat down and ordered an iced tea. I noticed that the guy sitting next to me was also wearing a badge from the conference. He lowered the newspaper he was reading and smiled my way. "Pretty bad energy in there, huh?"

I rolled my eyes. "The worst. So forced and schmoozy. I had to get out of there. Plus"—I shrugged—"I forgot to bring business cards."

He laughed and we started a conversation about Los Angeles, where we'd each grown up, and what we liked most about the podcast medium. It was an easy conversation, and just the kind I like—absent of an agenda. Before I knew it, forty minutes had passed, and I stood up to head to the first panel of the day.

He said, "Did you say you live in LA? We have an office here. Why don't you come have lunch with me next week?"

I hesitated. I didn't even know this guy's name or what he did for work. Was he also a podcast host? Today's panelist?

He smiled and handed me his card. Turns out, I'd been shooting the breeze with the head of marketing for Apple Podcasts.

When I tell this story, someone always asks me, how did you *do* that? How'd you make that happen?

I love this question because the answer is so simple: I didn't make anything happen. I wasn't trying to push for an outcome or strategize how I could meet the most sought-after person at the conference. I decided to step out of the energy of striving and lack that was surrounding me at the conference and step into wholeness. I found my way to what felt good right then and there in the present moment. While enjoying my iced tea, I met someone else who had chosen to find that energy of surrender too. The universe will always match us with whatever wavelength we're on.

That's it.

This story isn't about what I did; it's about who I was in the moment, what I projected onto the screen of the world in front of me. My energy. If you want to manifest abundance, it's not so much about what you do; it's about who you are. When you're vibrating at the high note of possibility, opportunities come to you. Really, think about the story I just told you—I left the conference and was minding my own business when the thing that everyone in that crowded hotel room desperately wanted fell directly into my lap.

The people who have created the most amazing lives, who've offered the world the most beautiful, innovative, generous, and inspired gifts, embody "flow," where they take action that isn't forced, fabricated, or pushy. And yet, it's deliberate. I'm no Michelangelo or Malcolm Gladwell, but allow me to apply this 90 to 10 percent rule in the context of my meeting the marketing head of Apple Podcasts. Instead of chasing the "how," I let the how happen, and from there I asked myself: *What's next? What's the next right step?* In this instance, it seemed obvious: accept his lunch invitation, which I did, and during our meal together, I spoke openly and honestly about what I was hoping to achieve with my podcast, which was to connect with and inspire women to live the lives they'd been dreaming of for years. And when he offered to feature my podcast on the Apple Podcast platform, I took the next right action: I said yes. On that serendipitous day in Anaheim, I met just the "right person" because I was a vibrational match for abundance. I wasn't hustling or false presenting; I showed up as me.

IT'S IN MOMENTS like this that you didn't plan ahead of time, you didn't anticipate, and you didn't expect to produce a higher volume of joy. It's in moments *unknown* that we often experience abundance.

If we allow it.

If we notice it.

So many of us are afraid of the unknown, almost allergic to it, because we falsely believe that repeating a day-to-day life of predictability is safer. We think that knowing what's up ahead is better than not knowing. We convince ourselves that feeling in control feels good.

Is that true?

Is predictability working for you?

Does control feel good?

Our minds tell us, *Yes, predictability and control are totally working for me!*, but our souls tell a different story. Our minds crave certainty, yet our souls delight in the unknown. Our souls live for those blow-your-hair-back moments where you exclaim, "Wow, I did not see that coming. And I'm so glad it did."

There's an amazing story that mindset coach Peter Crone shared with me. In his late twenties, he had gone through a devastating breakup, and he wanted this woman back so badly, to the point that he was physically sick. He obsessed: *Will she call? Where is she? Is she with someone else? Will I see her again?* It was just insanity. He had also lost his parents at a young age, so when the love of his life broke up with him, it triggered all that abandonment and brokenness. He knew it was unhealthy, but he couldn't live without her love and approval.

Weeks went by. No call, but the obsession still raged on. Then one day, he was sitting at his desk and ruminating again: *Where is she? Is she with someone else? Will I see her again? Will I ever have love like that again?*

As he tells the story, he was sitting at his IKEA desk and "I suddenly got the answer. I almost fell out of my chair because it was so simple. The answer was three words: *I don't know.* I don't know where she is. I don't know if she's with someone else. I don't know if I'll see her again. I don't know if I'll have love like that again. It still gives me chills now. I was oblivious to the fact that the nature of life is uncertainty. I was just like most people, constantly trying to figure it out. I realized the truth versus an opinion. And the truth was, we're all clueless. We don't know what's going to happen. No one's ever going to know what the future holds."

For the first time in his life, he found peace. He was okay not knowing. He was free.

What's crazy is that within fifteen minutes, his phone rang. And guess who it was? That's right, it was the ex-girlfriend. They hadn't spoken for about six weeks. She called him and she was crying, "I miss you so much."

Peter realized that he had been living with the illusion of loss, but in this moment, he dropped those fears over loss. He had never lost anything because he was already whole. Once that revelation was clear, he actually became available to her. She didn't know the epiphany he had just been through, of course, but because energetically the veil of constraint had just dropped, she was able to call him. He said from that moment on, "I knew there was nothing else to look for but true freedom."

Similarly to Peter, the biggest blessings of my life were things I did not see coming, that I bumped right into and surprised me, like moving into a new apartment building in Los Angeles after I'd pivoted my songwriting career to television and film, and meeting Ruthie, the older woman in the next-door unit who told me, "You will have good luck. Everyone who rents this apartment gets engaged the first year they live here. It's got a great mazel." Weird, I thought, and—she was right! When I met Ruthie's son soon after I moved in, I realized that I already knew him. Lowell and I had been introduced by tangential friends in Los Angeles. I didn't know him well, but because he stopped by his mother's apartment nearly every day to visit her, we quickly became acquainted. In time, we became good friends, and one day, my sister suggested the obvious: "Why don't you date Lowell? You get along so well." I had no good answer for her except to say—I thought I was looking for Patrick Dempsey on steroids. I didn't expect to date the guy next door.

I didn't expect to marry him either. And I did.

Another *I didn't see it coming* moment came ten days after my youngest daughter was born and a friend reached out to say congratulations. "What did you name her?"

"Maddie." I beamed at the new baby in my arms.

"I love that name," my friend said, "and so interesting because I know a gal named Maddie who sells advertising for podcasts, and I just told her about you over dinner because she's looking for people with inspirational stories who may be interested in launching a podcast. You should call her."

I appreciated the plug, but c'mon—I had a newborn and two other small children in the house. My hands were more than full. I had no business starting a podcast, did I? I ignored my friend's nudging for about a week, until it hit me: Why not? Why not call and see what greets me on the other end of the line? And guess what? The podcast that Maddie and I talked about over lunch became the first version of my podcast, *Don't Keep Your Day Job*, which encouraged listeners to create a career based on doing what they loved most—baking, painting, dancing, whatever *it* was for them. I hadn't seen myself as a podcaster before—I was a songwriter, right?—and I didn't know the first thing about how to create one. The kickoff episode that I recorded in my closet was messy and unrefined—I hated the sound of my voice—but listeners seemed to like it, and that small, imperfect podcast that I started on a whim had over a million downloads within the first year. If I hadn't pursued the unknown eight years ago, I wouldn't be anywhere close to where I am today. The moments that make our lives magical are a series of unplanned, beautiful gifts that we didn't foresee, that we didn't force, that we didn't insist on happening, that we didn't predict. Our minds like to tell us that happiness is about life going our way, and that "thought" only sets us up for disappointment because rarely, if ever, do things unfold as we predicted or attempted to control.

> **Think of all the ways your life has already been blessed. Is this because you "figured it out" ahead of time? Or has it been blessed by beautiful synchronicity?**

BUT WHEN, WHERE, AND HOW?

When I talk on my podcast about letting go of control and embracing the unknown where our greatest expansion lies, several versions of the same question inevitably pop up in the chat: But when, where, and how?! This query is usually followed by others, like: If I don't *make* things happen, how can I expect anything to happen at all? If I don't push myself or exert great effort, how can I expect to reach my goal?

Our brains tell us that we must control, overdo, and force things to happen, and that is the big lie. Furthermore, every time we ask questions like, "Where will the money come from? When will my income double? How will I lose weight? When will I find the love of my life?" we are focusing on lack, on what we don't have. By focusing on the thing you want but don't have, you tune the radio dial *away* from receiving it. I said it in the first pages of this book—the law of attraction holds us back from allowing in more because the radio station of asking and attracting is very different from the station for receiving. It's like listening to the Oldies station and getting frustrated that there are no Adele songs playing. You won't find Adele on the Oldies channel; you must change the channel. That said, asking is not without merit. Asking for what we want is important because it forces us to become super clear on what we most desire—but after the ask, we must turn our attention away from focusing on the desire, on what is not there, yet. Additionally, we must turn our attention away from *how* we will fulfill our desire.

You see, most of us were taught to set goals, to dream our dreams, and then reverse-engineer how to achieve them. Have the goal first and then figure out how to get there. The problem with this process is that so many of us get stuck on how it's going to happen, and that's not our job—the *how*. Our part is to simply dream the dream and then take one actionable step forward and trust that it will get us where we need to go. Before I started my songwriting business, I came across that article in *Billboard* magazine about musicians who were licensing their music to TV and film, writing songs for shows like *Grey's Anatomy* and *Dawson's Creek*. I had no idea how I could also license my music in this way. I couldn't see all the steps that would get me there, but I was inspired to take at least one step in that direction. I googled the names of television executives. That was step one. Then I followed that action by making cold calls. That was step two. Then I sent my Mochas and Music email blast. That was step three. In many ways, I was walking blind, but I was moving forward. I was taking steps and trusting that they would lead me in the direction I was meant to go. And with each step, I became more inspired, more encouraged and excited by the process. I was excited by where it may eventually lead, yes, but also—and maybe more so—I was excited by how I felt in the moment. I woke up every morning feeling pumped by what I might create that day, what new opportunity awaited in the next hour, how I might be surprised around the corner. Moment to moment, I was having fun! When we stop ruminating on the "how" and repeating those old thoughts and feelings of doubt and limitation, we create space for new energy to move through us—the abundant energy of the universe, the energy of creativity, collaboration, expansion, and wholeness. When we change the dial, the world responds; it attunes to the new song that we are singing, and before we know it, life delivers a new path forward, one that is often surprising. When you stop operating from a place of control and predictability, new possibilities appear seemingly out of nowhere, and that's what our souls desire most—to play in the unknown, where all potentials exist.

MOVE TWO DEGREES

It's important to remember that change isn't instant; it's a process made possible by taking incremental steps forward, and sometimes by only a matter of degrees. Let's say a boat is clocked to head to a specific destination and it changes course by only two degrees. If it were to continue twenty more miles, and twenty more after that, and again and again, that boat would wind up at the shore of a completely different continent than the one it had originally set sail for. All because of an incremental change of two degrees. Often, when we think of creating change, we think it's all or nothing, and we put immense pressure on ourselves to see quick results. It's easy to fall into this all-too-common trap, thinking that we must make giant changes in order to see a shift. Incremental and sustainable change happens best when we stop overthinking, when we instead engage in intentional steps forward in a manner of degrees. What feels good, what feels full and satisfying right now? Lean into that. *That's a shift of two degrees.* Breathe deeply. *That's a shift of two degrees.* Notice what is in front of you, right here, right now. *That's a shift of two degrees.*

Intentionally notice your thoughts. Where are they leading you? *That's a shift of two degrees.*

Instead of pushing yourself to block out your calendar to make *big* shifts by Friday, allow yourself to notice when you've shifted just a little. Challenge yourself to incrementally think, feel, and respond differently, and the more you make this a practice, the sooner you will automatically memorize a new space where there is a pause between the notes, and where you shift beyond your thinking mind to the frequency of abundance, and where you're likely to bump into something magical by moving only two degrees.

LESS CONTROL. MORE RIDE.

So how do you do that? How do you let go? How do you trust that the contrast in your life is leading you in the right direction? How do you turn the dial away from limitation?

What did I tell you? The *how* is not your job.

Your next actionable step forward is to *be*.

To bring yourself back to the present moment and be in it.

When you consider our culture of never enough-ness, we're no different. We're on the never-enough train, which means we're always traveling toward the future, searching for more. To turn the dial away from limitation, you must look no further than where you are *in this moment* and notice what's good. Go ahead, do it, look at your life right now. Feel into it. Feel into your belly. What feels good? What feels full and satisfying right now? When I challenge myself with this question, one of the first things I feel is the sunlight coming in through a window. The sun feels full. On other days, I may stop to notice one of my adorable kittens stumbling across the floor. That feels full. As I was writing this paragraph, I took a bite of an apple. That single crunchy, tangy bite filled me. In every moment, there is beauty and wonder and love and grace and kindness and patience and forgiveness and peace and inspiration and healing to behold. It's there. Not all of it at once, but something good is there.

It's like looking at a piece of sheet music. There are notes on the page; *also* there is the pause between the notes. What most often makes a piece of music beautiful is the pause in between the crescendo and the following three notes. It's the silence, the music of stillness, that our ear delightfully attunes. Can you hear the pause between the notes within your own life? What's happening in that space? What do you hear? What do you feel? It's within that space where we meet our true self, our infinite, abundant self. When we take the time to notice the pause between the notes, they start building on one another and expanding our opening to receive.

**Can you hear the pause between the notes?
What's happening in that space?**

TAKE A WALK

Steve Jobs was famous for taking two walks a day without his phone. And it was on those walks, he claimed, that he would get his biggest creative downloads, his biggest ideas and inspiration. I challenge you to similarly "take a walk" two times a day, during which you intentionally stop what you're doing and focus on the moment. Take a deep breath and invite the feeling of satisfaction to rise within you. What feels good right now? What is filling you up in this very moment? It could be a hot cup of coffee, the conversation you just had with a close friend, how your body feels in your clothes today, or gazing across the street at your neighbor's beautiful rose garden. Look around and feel into the moment. Is there something happening right now that you have no control over, that you didn't see coming, that you didn't anticipate or expect or force, *and* that feels good? The surprising, exciting, inspiring, and *I feel grateful* moments are the ones to notice. As you make this a practice, you will soon realize how each moment holds a special kind of fullness, and as you continue this practice, you will teach yourself to notice satisfaction. As you do, your internal dial will shift toward the channel of receiving where there's nothing to pull; there's nothing to force or push. You will automatically move in the direction of abundance.

What feels good right now?

15.

YOU ARE A SOUL.
YOU HAVE A BODY.

WHEN WE WERE driving home from school the other day, my daughter Eliza, who is now ten years old, said to me, "Mommy, you know how I play Roblox and they have all these worlds?"

"Are you talking about the metaverse?" The metaverse is the notion that there are multiple realities and multiple paths—a concept that I assumed would be far from the interests of my daughters.

"Yes," she answered, impressed that I was speaking her language. She continued, "I realized something about us as humans."

"What's that?"

"I realized that I am a soul and that Eliza is my avatar."

I nearly ran off the road, her insights were so profound. "Go on," I encouraged her.

"Since Eliza is just my avatar, I can change her anytime I want. I can change her hair color and clothes, and I can control what she does and where she goes. But my insides stay the same."

I couldn't have said it better myself. In fact, Eliza could probably have written this book.

When my daughters were born, I gave them names: Eliza, Madeleine, and Gabrielle. I dressed them up in adorable dresses and combed their hair. But before all that, they were already themselves. They were bright, light, limitless souls who decided to come to Earth to learn a few things. We are *some of the one*, some of the infinite Oneness. We are intrinsically whole. As Rabbi Aaron says, "We are someone, because we are some of Infinite Oneness."

My daughter's insight that we are each an avatar on the outside and a soul on the inside is the last thing I encourage you to ponder as you close this book and get back to your life. In this 3-D space, what is your avatar? What is the role you're playing? What kind of "somebody" are you? And is that version of yourself in alignment with your soul? Is it congruent and authentic to *you*?

Without realizing it, most of us spend a large part of our lives identifying with our avatar, the character and role we learned to play based on unconscious limiting beliefs, false messaging, and codependent people-pleasing. But, as you now know, your avatar is not *you*. It's a projection, one you can change at any time or abandon all together. Because in this corner of the metaverse, you don't need to identify with an outdated role that no longer fits, if it ever did. The winners in this game remember that their greatest strength is not what is perceived on the outside but what lies within: authenticity. When you show up every day with presence, with love and kindness, and with a life force energy that is unique to *you* and resonates with the symphony of the universe, you cannot lose. In fact, this is when the walls of limitation fall away and all that's left is a rainbow door that leads to expansion and infinite possibility.

And finally, I want to leave you with a prayer. It's a part of the daily morning prayers in Jewish tradition in which you ask God to make you like a rooster. *A rooster? Why, what is this prayer? What is this about? Why would I want to be like a rooster?*

One day recently, a Holocaust survivor explained this prayer to me. She said the rooster is the very first one on the farm to understand that darkness is the beginning of light. Just when the night can't get any darker, in that split second, a millisecond after it's the darkest it can be, the rooster crows. "Wake up. Wake up. Because the light is here. Because the dawn is about to break." The woman who shared this with me—her name was Esther Youngreis (may her memory be a blessing)—passed away. She said, "When I was in a concentration camp at five years old, my father would say, 'Be like a rooster.'" And she said, "I didn't really know what that meant until years later. George W. Bush was flying on *Air Force One* to the opening of the Holocaust Memorial Museum in Jerusalem and asked me to be his guest.

"I accepted the invitation, and when we were flying back to America, I fell asleep, and he tapped me on the shoulder to wake me up. He said, 'Esther, I'm sorry to wake you, but I want you to look out the window.' I looked out the window and he said, 'Do you know where you are? Right now you're flying with the president of the United States in *Air Force One*, coming from Jerusalem, flying over Germany.'"

Esther understood then what it meant to be like a rooster. Wait for the light. It will come; it will arrive without fail. Trust and believe.

And now it's time for you to follow her lead.

It's time to say, "Okay, enough's enough. What could I create if I got out of my resistance and out of my ego and I changed the radio station? How could my very existence bring more love and light to the world?" For we are all part of the infinite Oneness, and we all were put here to make the world a more beautiful place by adding our unique vibration. The more we return to our true Self, our soul, the more abundant we'll be, and the more abundance we'll create for the world to give and receive.

ACKNOWLEDGMENTS

I sat down to write these acknowledgments and was flooded with a list of people who are so dear and important to me, and who have helped me become who I am and allowed me to write this book.

But before I thank these incredible souls, I want to stop and acknowledge myself. Yep, that's right—I want to say thank you, Cathy. It's so important that we pull over to the side of our lives and celebrate our *self*. It's so important that we recognize how far we've come. The truth is that happiness is an inside job, and the happiest, most loving people in the world don't need other people's approval because they RSVP to their own party, and it takes a certain amount of humility and honesty and integrity to raise our hand to do what we came into the world to do—and then to acknowledge that we had the courage to do it.

When I look back at myself at five years old, at twelve years old, and at twenty years old, it truly is remarkable that I am where I am today, and I'm so incredibly proud of all the work and all the ways that I have continued to keep reaching for love and light.

Next, I want to acknowledge my parents for bringing me into this world.

My mom taught me what it means to be creative and to have incredible empathy. She has the capacity to feel more than anyone I know. And she always encouraged me to play and to prioritize being messy and alive over being perfect.

My dad, who recently passed, overcame childhood trauma and significant hearing loss and was determined to make a purpose-driven life for himself and to provide for his family. He modeled incredible resilience, showing me that we all have an amazing capacity to grow and believe in big dreams, and to believe in ourselves. While there were many years when things felt broken, he eventually became my teacher. I also want to thank my step-mom, Marti, for loving my dad to the point where he became the best version of himself. At the end, there was no pain, only love, and my one regret is that I didn't open my heart to him sooner and receive more of his care. After all, that is what we are here to do: to receive love in abundance. May we all have the courage to open our hearts.

Next, I want to acknowledge my grandmother, Betty, who gave me the tenacity to believe that there was nothing I couldn't do. She had incredible gratitude and was in love with joy and finding joy. Her husband, my grandfather Ben, lived life to the fullest, and even though I never met him, I feel as though he's always watched over me and that he taught me the power of dance.

I want to acknowledge my sister, Barbara, who is loyal, kind, and forgiving, and who always has my back. She was my first friend, and she would do anything for me. I learned so much about forgiveness and compassion from her, and there are really no words to sum up what having her in my life has brought to me.

I want to acknowledge my husband, Lowell, who truly has given me so much unconditional love, and who loved me back to life. His consistent, grounding kindness and acceptance gave me my wings. My capacity to be-

come an incredible manifester is due in part to the stability and safety pro-
vided by his protective, loyal heart.

I want to thank my three children, Gabrielle, Eliza, and Maddie. There
are no words to capture the joy and radiance that you each bring into my
life. With each of your births, I felt that I had more power and capacity to
live up to my potential. You inspire me. You are pure magic, and everything
I do is for you.

I owe so much of this book and who I am to the greatest teacher, rabbi,
and mentor in my life, Rabbi David Aaron. You have shown me the world
through new lenses and given me a way to make sense of everything. You
taught me that I was a masterpiece, a piece of the master. You are the most
loving, kind soul I've ever known, and knowing you has made me a better
person.

I also want to thank Rabbi Binny Freedman and his wife, Doreet, for
their wisdom and for helping shape me into who I am; Rabbi Yossi Shapiro,
for your goodness, kindness, friendship, and wisdom; Rabbi Bengi Levine
and his family, for being an example of unconditional love and wisdom; and
Rabbi Seidenfeld and Lolly, for being family and for giving me so much love
and adding so much to my life.

I want to also thank my best friend, Jenny, and her beautiful family. To
have a friend like you is magical, and it's a joy to walk this path with someone as special, generous, and kindhearted as you.

Next, I want to thank Emma Kikuchi, who has been with me since the
beginning of the podcast. She is the easiest person to be around, always generous and kind and eager to help. Her sure-footedness and can-do attitude
allowed me to create, and I'm so grateful to have her in my life. She was
a huge help with this book and never complained, even though I sent her
many things throughout the journey, sometimes at the last minute; whatever good comes from this book is, in large part, due to her.

ACKNOWLEDGMENTS

I want to thank Samantha Rose for her dedicated editorial support, and for going through these pages line by line to shine my words into more coherent golden nuggets. It was my pleasure to work with you.

I want to thank my publisher, Libby McGuire; my agent, Joe Veltre; my first editor, Leah Miller; and Samantha Weiner and the rest of the team at Simon & Schuster for being completely and totally awesome, and for helping me put this book into the world while being extremely patient about the time it took for me to get it right.

I want to thank the women on my team, Ezgi and Jen, for always believing in my dreams and helping me to execute them.

I want to thank all the incredible guests on my podcast whose words have made it into these pages. You have taught me so much and enhanced my life in such a tremendous way. It is such an honor to have one-on-one conversations with you. There is no greater gift than giving someone wisdom and a different perspective on life, and you have all been so significant in that way.

Finally, I want to thank all the incredible souls who have listened to my podcast and supported me along this journey. This wouldn't have been possible without the love you've given me for the past eight years. I hope you continue to spread your love and light throughout the world and to open your hearts to the abundance of the Universe.

MY GIFT TO YOU

CathyHeller.com/More

Scan this QR code to unlock a treasure trove of resources like guided med-
itations, affirmation cards, journal prompts, and other delightful surprises
designed to support your abundance journey.

For my dad, Philip Edward Heller, who passed away as I was completing this manuscript and who had a wonderful heart and truly felt abundant as he appreciated the most abundant aspects of life. He taught me to celebrate life, be resilient, and love with all my heart. May his memory be a blessing. I found this essay he wrote, and I wanted to share an excerpt of it with you.

LESSONS FROM THE JETTY

BY DR. PHIL HELLER

The ocean invites the soul to its sanctuary each and every day. In prayer I thank God for the blessings bestowed upon me, which, aside from my home, include my wife, two daughters, and the surrounding family and friends. The prayer and the beach provide a moment of solace. My beach has a rock jetty that invades the ocean, bringing me closer to God. As I walk to the ocean the light is beginning to appear and the salty mist gently brushes my face. The clean sound of the water hitting the rocks offers a sense of freshness as the day begins. The pelicans sit attentively on a nearby dock worn by storms of the past. The sandpipers run along the beach and the seagulls await the light to search for their daily sustenance.

As the symphony of dawn begins, a quiet consumes the beach and the red ball of fire starts its ascent to the heavens. Wonder pervades as the sun rises up and the ocean goes out to greet the day's light. This experience brings hope of a new day while centering me to face the experiences that life will bring in the hours to come. To stand on the jetty is to be in nature's classroom as she reveals her lessons to one who is willing to learn.

Each day has a regularity. The sun rises and the waves roll, endorsing the consistency of life on which we depend. As our hearts beat rhythmically, so does the ocean. The ocean has its moods. The water can be so flat that dolphins are observed engaged in a ballet with the waves.

The rocks of the jetty refuse to move in their permanence. The fixture creates a sense of security reminiscent of the Rock of Gibraltar. Wooden structures are victims to hurricanes, but the jetty can be a steadfast model for integrity and strength. There is little doubt that it will be there tomorrow. The same security lies in the rhythm of the tide and the rising of the sun. These are truths in which one can believe. It is without question that this is God's creation.

When I complete my prayers, I am so enmeshed in thought that I can leave the beach without noticing its grandeur. As I leave, I make a point to turn back and take the time to enjoy God's majesty. It is a breathtaking moment to view what I came to experience. Stop and smell the roses. The rest of the world will wait.

ABOUT THE AUTHOR

CATHY HELLER is a dynamic transformational coach, spiritual guide, meditation teacher, and inspirational speaker dedicated to helping individuals find ease, joy, and fulfillment in their lives. As the host of the *Abundant Ever After* podcast and author of the empowering book *Don't Keep Your Day Job: How to Turn Your Passion into Your Career*, Cathy inspires her audience to pursue their dreams and live authentically.

Cathy's passion lies in helping people find joy and meaning beyond material wealth, and she has transformed the lives of hundreds of thousands through her teachings. Her work encompasses meditation, Jewish mysticism, and business strategies, empowering individuals to expand their potential and make a positive impact on the world. Proud mother to three daughters and four Persian cats, Cathy embodies a beautiful balance of creativity, family, and purpose.

MY REFLECTIONS AND TAKEAWAYS